SCIENCE FACTS!

How to Surf a VOLCANO

And Other Incredible Ideas About Earth Science

William Potter

Richard Watson

ARCTURUS

This edition published in 2025 by Arcturus Publishing Limited
26/27 Bickels Yard, 151–153 Bermondsey Street,
London SE1 3HA

Author: William Potter
Illustrator: Richard Watson
Consultants: Meriel Lland and Michael Leach
Editor: Lydia Halliday
Designer: Sarah Fountain
Managing Editor: Joe Harris
Managing Designer: Jessica Holliland

ISBN: 978-1-3988-5646-2
CH011601US
Supplier 29, Date. 0525, PI 00009060

Printed in Malaysia

Contents

Professor Katzenstein's Engaging Exploration of

Earth Science

We're really lucky living on Earth. Its **TEMPERATURE**, **ATMOSPHERE**, and abundant **WATER** are just right for life.
And there's chocolate and bananas, too!

You'd better pack some chocolate and bananas, Scooter, since we're going on a journey that will take us to the highest mountain, highest lake, deepest part of the ocean, and even the Earth's core.
Will this be enough?
On second thought, chocolate will melt in the center of the Earth.

We'll also look at the forces that affect the shape of the planet, how moving plates can raise mountains, how wind can wear down rocks, and how water can carve canyons ...
Can you feel the bridge swinging?
I can feel my knees trembling!

How do you know all this stuff about Earth, Professor?
You could say I have a planet-sized brain, Scooter.

Before we head out, I'd like you to sign this.
I didn't know you were a fan.

This is an agreement to show that you understand the risks of joining me on this Earth Science adventure.
Risks?!
The Earth is a dynamic place, Scooter. We'll be getting close to active **VOLCANOES**, **AVALANCHES**, **HURRICANES**, and **EARTHQUAKES**.

Could we look at Earth from a less dangerous place, like from another planet?
Don't worry, Scooter, you're in a safe pair of paws.

No harm will come to ... **WHOA!**
FLUMP!

Home Sweet Home

(Anatomy of Earth)

How to Build a Planet
What are you doing, Scooter?
FWFF!
FWFF!

I'm inflating the Earth. It's exhausting!
Let me help.

Of course, the **REAL** Earth took a lot longer to form.
FWFF!
FWFF!
Um, Professor...

Billions of years ago, dust and gases were pulled together to form our planet and all the Solar System.
FWFF!
FWFF!
I think it's big enough now...

FWFF!
FWFF!
Earth was really hot at first, but it cooled down, and oceans and air began to cover the surface.
So that's how it started. How will it end?

BANG!
I shouldn't have asked ...

Gravity began to pull on the dust and gas, and it formed a spinning disk with the Sun in the middle. About 4.5 billion years ago, smaller pieces of matter bumped into each other around the Sun. These clumped together to form the planets, including the rocky planet Earth.

At first, Earth was covered in **magma** or molten rock. Over millions of years, this cooled and became solid layers over a heavy molten core. During its formation, a large impact is thought to have led to a piece of Earth breaking away and forming the Moon.

As the Earth grew, so did its gravitational pull. The gravity captured the gases released from volcanic activity, and an **atmosphere** developed. Asteroids brought water, and thc oceans grew.

Bacteria added oxygen to the atmosphere over time, until the planet was able to support a variety of life.

How to Figure Out Earth's Birthday

A new addition for your rock collection?
Yes, I found this pretty pebble on the beach.

This is GRANITE.
I've named it PINKY.

Which is your oldest rock?
This one, named Stripy. It's two years old.

I think you'll find it's MUCH older ... maybe billions of years old.
Gasp!

Should I offer it to a museum?

Some elements found in rocks are **radioactive.** These go through a process called **decay,** where they lose atomic particles called **neutrons** and change into a different form called an **isotope.** This change can take millions of years. The more an element has changed into a new isotope, the older it is.

By comparing the amounts of different isotopes in a rock sample, scientists can work out how old it is. This method is called **radiometric dating.**

By dating all these different rocks, scientists have estimated that the age of Earth is **4.54 billion years.**

Into the Core

It's almost 140 times the pressure on land, but the Borer should be strong enough.
"Should be?!" We're going to be squished!
Now, we're floating!
We've reach the **OUTER CORE**. This is a liquid layer of mostly **IRON** and **NICKEL**.
Inner core
Outer core
Mantle
Crust
And, finally, the Earth's solid **INNER CORE**!
The temperature here is about 5,200 °C (9,400 °F), almost as hot as the Sun's surface, but the metals don't melt due to the enormous pressure.
It's good to be back safely after that amazing trip, but I have one question, Professor.
What's that?
WARNING! IN REALITY, ANYONE WHO DUG THEIR WAY TO THE EARTH'S CORE WOULD GET CRUSHED (AND IT WOULD MAKE A MESS OF YOUR GARDEN).
Who's going to fill in the big hole we made?

How to Flatten the Earth

The distance from the center of the Earth to the surface is 21 km (13 miles) greater at the equator than it is at the poles, a difference of just 0.3 per cent.

If you measured from the center of the Earth rather than sea level, Mount Chimborazo in Ecuador would be the highest point on Earth, not Mount Everest!

As the Earth spins, a **centrifugal force** pushes outward from the Earth's **axis** (an imagined line between the poles). This makes the force of gravity weaker at the equator than the poles, and it means you will weigh slightly less there by a very, very small amount.

How to Survive Space Weather
Wow!
I promised I'd show you the **NORTHERN LIGHTS**, and here they are!

They're amazing!
But what makes all these shimmering lights in the sky?

It's caused by the solar wind hitting gases in the air, and is thanks to **EARTH'S MAGNETIC FIELD**.

If it wasn't for Earth's magnetic field, we wouldn't be here.
You mean there wouldn't be any lights?

There wouldn't be any **ATMOSPHERE**!
The solar wind could blast away Earth's atmosphere like it did on the planet Mars.

What do you think of that, Scooter?
I'm blown away!

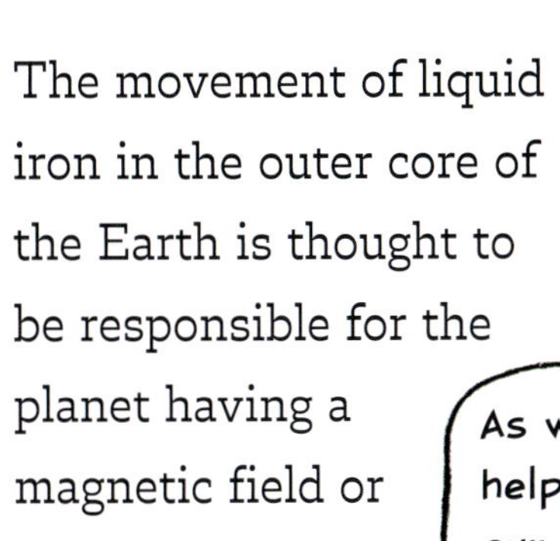

The movement of liquid iron in the outer core of the Earth is thought to be responsible for the planet having a magnetic field or **magnetosphere**.

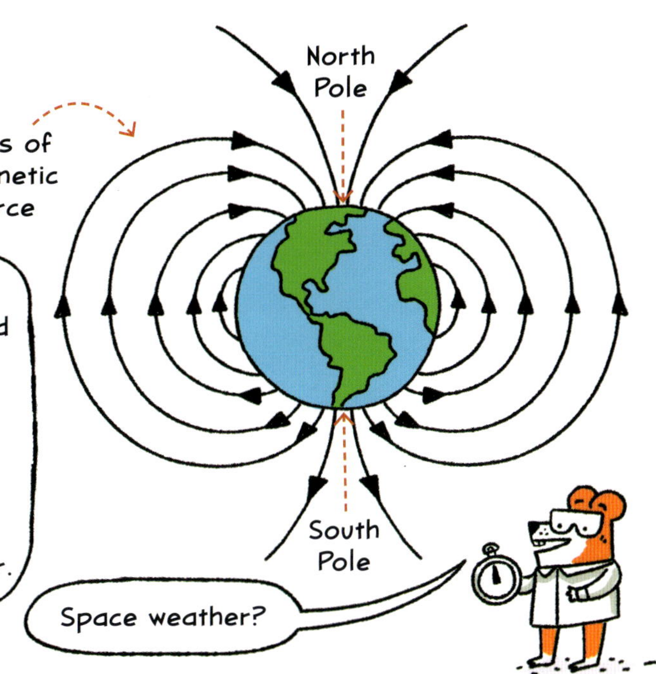

The outer layer of the Sun produces a **solar wind**—streams of electrically charged particles. When they reach Earth, most bounce off the magnetic field, but some are directed to the poles.

Here, they hit gases in the upper atmosphere and produce streams of light called **aurorae—aurora borealis (northern lights)**, and **aurora australis (southern lights)**.

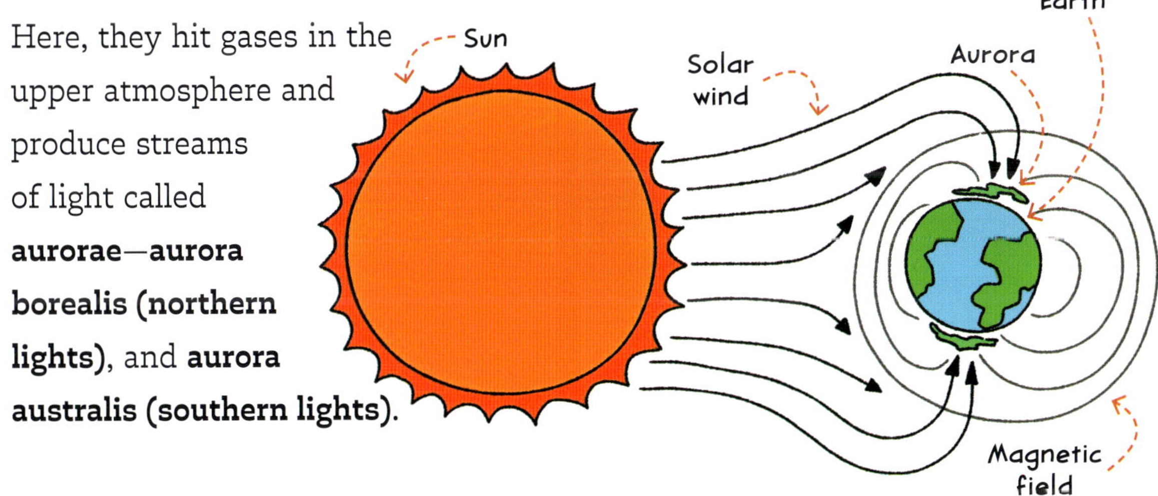

If Earth was not shielded by the magnetic field, the solar wind would hit the Earth, causing harmful radiation and the disappearance of the atmosphere (the gases around our planet).

How to Be Crusty
Ta-da! My pie is ready!
Good job, Chef Scooter!

I call it my Earth pie, crusty and filling, like our planet.

What's inside it?
I filled it with vegetables that grow in the earth, like potatoes and carrots.

Excellent.
I baked a thin crust like Earth's, too.

Good idea. What's it made of?
Soil.

Bleugh!
Bleugh!

The Earth is covered by a **crust**, a rocky layer that moves over the denser **mantle** below. This crust is relatively thin. If the Earth was an apple, the crust would be as thin as its skin.

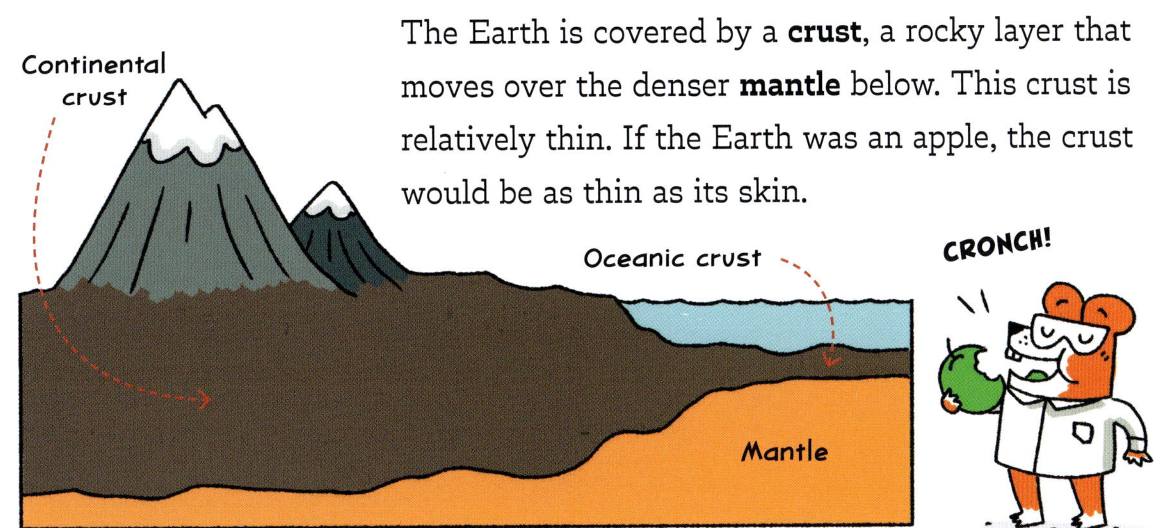

The **continental crust** is the topmost layer on land. It is mostly made from rocks called **granite**. This layer can extend up to 70 km (44 miles) thick below mountain ranges.

The **oceanic crust** is the layer at the bottom of the seas and is mostly made from volcanic rock called **basalt**. This crust is denser but thinner, just 5 km (3 miles) thick in places. It is much younger than the continental crust, 200 million years old at most. This crust is covered by marine sediment, mud, and sea life that sinks to the ocean bed.

Rock Stars

The rocks that make up the Earth are made of one or more substances called **minerals**. There are about 4,000 known minerals, but only 30 are common on Earth's surface.

There are three common Earth minerals ... **QUARTZ**, **FELDSPAR**, and **OLIVINE**!

Whoops!

KREESH!

Minerals are identified by their characteristics, including their color, hardness, how much they reflect light ... and how they break.

Some are easy to find and durable, perfect for building or making tools. Some sparkle and are collected as gems. Some are rare and shiny metals, and used for jewelry.

Elemental minerals are those made up of just one substance called an **element**. These include **gold**, **silver**, **copper**, and **platinum**. Some, like gold, can be very rare and are treasured for their look and properties. Platinum is rarer than gold and is also used in jewelry, as well as computer components and vehicle fuel cells.

The rarest mineral on Earth is an orange gemstone called **KYAWTHUITE**. Only one small sample of it has been found.

Where is it, Scooter?

Um, I lost it.

Compound minerals are those made up of more than one element. These include **sulfides** (containing sulfur), **oxides** (containing oxygen), and **silicates** (containing silicon). Silicate minerals make up about 90 per cent of the Earth's crust by weight.

How to Sparkle
What do you think of my new diamond bracelet, Professor?

Diamonds are precious gemstones, the hardest mineral found on Earth!
I must be paying you too much ...

It wasn't expensive. I bought it from a street market.

May I take a closer look?
You can try it on if you like.

I'm sorry to tell you, Scooter, but these are not real diamonds.

They may not be diamonds but I still think it's pretty.
That's what's important, Scooter.
If it makes you happy, it's priceless.

Gemstones are some of the most prized minerals found in the Earth's crust, admired for their shine, toughness, and rarity. Most gems are **crystal** forms of minerals, with flat sides and regular geometric shapes.

A gem should be durable so it is not easily scratched. Expert gem cutters give the stones sharper edges and polished sides called **facets**, which reflect the light and make them more sparkly.

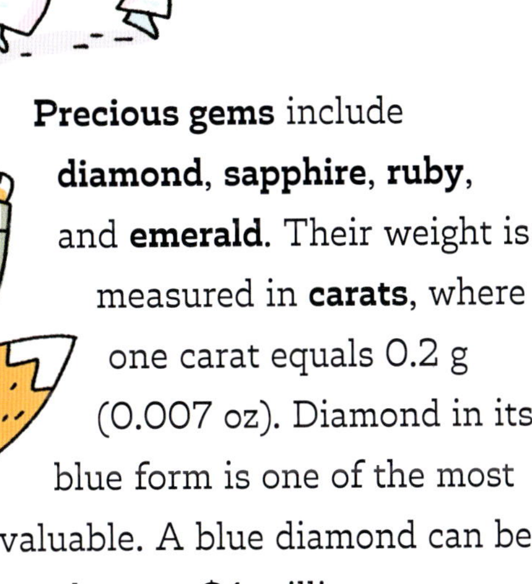

Precious gems include **diamond**, **sapphire**, **ruby**, and **emerald**. Their weight is measured in **carats**, where one carat equals 0.2 g (0.007 oz). Diamond in its blue form is one of the most valuable. A blue diamond can be worth up to $4 million per carat.

All other gems are considered to be **semiprecious**. These include **topaz**, **opal**, and **jade**.

How to Collect Lava
Just look at this, Scooter, the Earth in action!
MAGMA from the upper mantle, emerging as LAVA ...
I've got my bucket for collecting samples!

Scooter, that's a plastic bucket. Lava reaches temperatures up to 1,200 °C (2,200 °F).
It will melt through your bucket in a flash.
Oh.

What about your bucket?
This is steel and filled with cold water.

Here's some lava. I'll use the hammer to scoop some up and drop it in the water to cool.

This is lava that has cooled and has begun turning into IGNEOUS ROCK.

If only we had a way of collecting samples of this, too ...

Magma is liquid or semiliquid rock under Earth's surface. When it erupts or flows onto the surface or underwater, it becomes **lava**. When this cools, it crystallizes and becomes **igneous rock**. There are three common types of igneous rock.

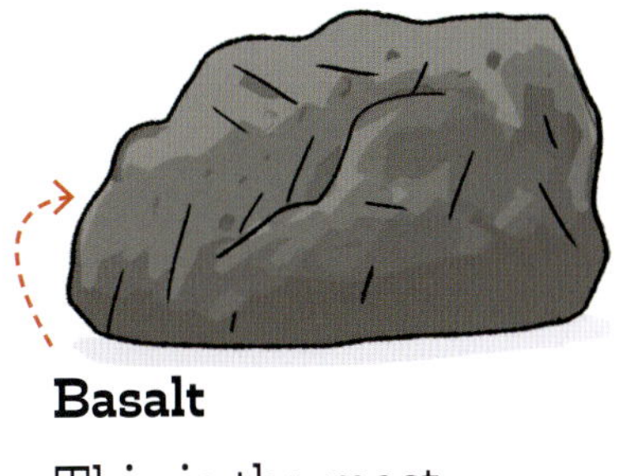

Basalt
This is the most common igneous rock found in the oceanic crust. It is also used in construction and as a base for roads.

Granite
This is the most common rock in the Earth's continental crust. It can be gray, white, pink, or black and is used in buildings.

Professor, look, I'm super-strong!

Pumice
This is a very light rock produced in volcanic eruptions. Full of air bubbles, this rock can float on water. It is used in cleaning products.

How to
Carve a
Temple
Professor!

Yes?
Oh, I was going to show you my sandcastle ...
Sandcastle?

Would you like to see something amazing built from sand?
Yes, please!

This is Abu Simbel in Egypt, a temple built for the pharaoh Ramses II over 3,000 years ago.
Is it really made from sand?

It's carved from SANDSTONE, a SEDIMENTARY ROCK made from grains of sand that became cemented together.
Wow!

I need to up my game ...

Sandstone is a **sedimentary rock**. Most of the rock seen on Earth's surface is sedimentary.

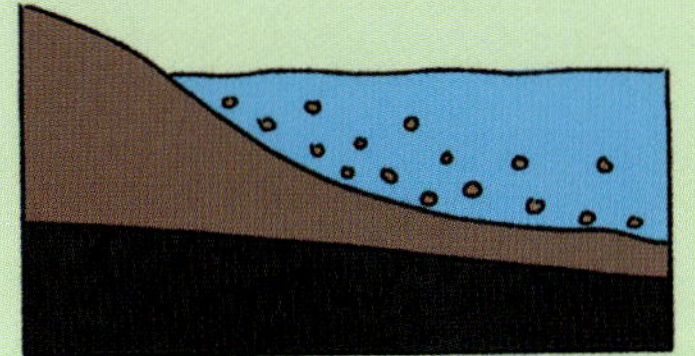

Sedimentary rock is made up of fine grains worn from other rocks. These grains are moved about by wind and water and often end up in the sea.

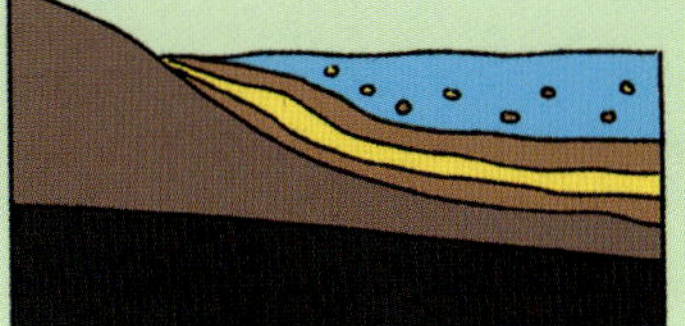

Over time, these grains pile up and become **compacted** by the weight of the grains and water above.

The grains are cemented together to become new layers of rock. This process, called **lithification**, may take millions of years.

Sedimentary rocks include:

Sandstone

This rock contains a lot of the mineral quartz. It can be worn away by weather or carved into buildings.

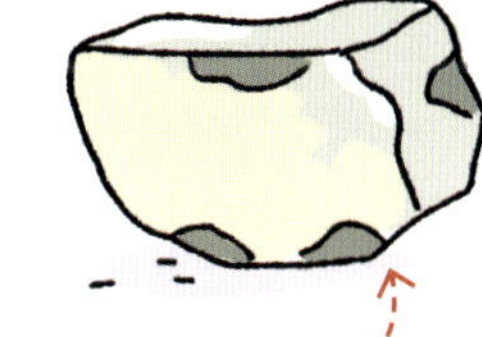

Limestone

Most of this rock is made from the shells and skeletal remains of sea creatures. Limestone can be dissolved in acidic water, leaving holes in the rock.

Shale

Shale is one of the most common sedimentary rocks. It spilts easily into thin layers. Many fossils have been found in these layers.

Bryce Canyon

Bryce Canyon in Utah, USA, is a spectacular example of sedimentary rock (sandstone and shale) that has been eroded over millions of years by wind and water to form spires.

How to Sculpt like Michelangelo
Thank you for posing for me, Dr. Ringtail.
How is your sculpture going, Scooter?

SIGH! I'll never be as good as the sculptor MICHELANGELO.
Your sculpture is very ... expressive.

If you want to be like Michelangelo, you need to use MARBLE.

Marble is a METAMORPHIC ROCK changed due to heat and pressure in the Earth's crust.
And now Scooter is going to change it into a work of art!
Hooray!

Hours later ...
How is it going, Scooter?
CHOK!
CHOK!

SIGH! I've only scratched it!

Metamorphic rock is rock that is affected by changing pressure and temperatures underground.

This alters its properties, including the minerals that make it up.

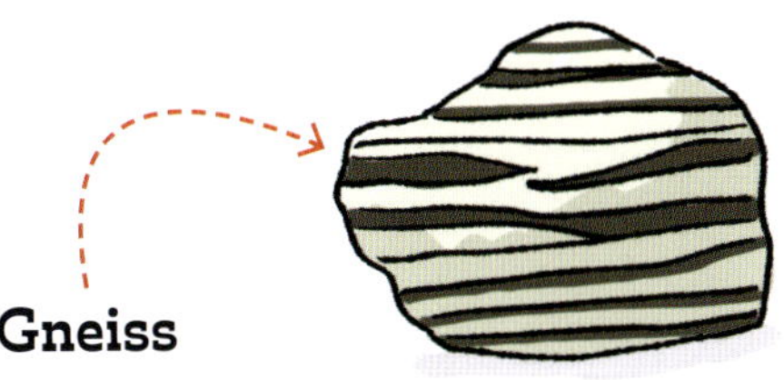

Gneiss

This metamorphic rock is formed under high temperatures and pressure. It features bands of minerals in several shades and is used for flooring and gravestones.

Slate

Slate is formed from clay and volcanic ash under low temperatures and pressure. Since it easily splits into flat sheets, slate is often used in roof tiles, floors, and work surfaces.

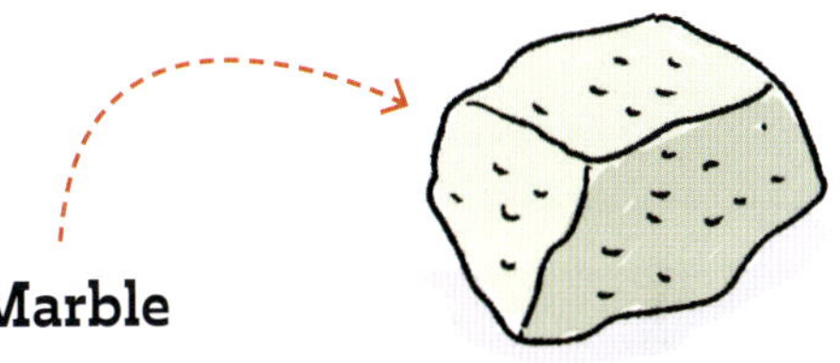

Marble

Marble is made when mountains are formed, with limestone transformed through underground heat and pressure. Marble is prized for decorating buildings and for sculpture.

How to Fire Up a Fossil
I'm going to start a fossil collection.
Another collection? Do we have room?

There's space in the Scooter Museum.
You mean your bedroom?
Museum

I can give you a fossil.
This is coal. I was hoping for a dinosaur.
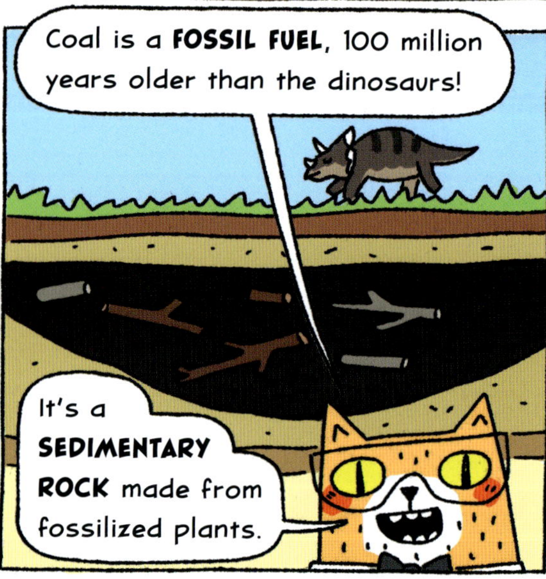
Coal is a **FOSSIL FUEL**, 100 million years older than the dinosaurs!
It's a **SEDIMENTARY ROCK** made from fossilized plants.

Don't we need coal for fuel?
Burning fossil fuels is going out like the dinosaurs.
We need to use more **RENEWABLE ENERGY SOURCES**, like wind, water, and solar power.
seum
Then I'll just keep this in my museum.

Coal, **oil**, and **gas** are **fossil fuels** found underground. They are the result of prehistoric plants and other organisms dying and being buried millions of years ago.

Coal

Coal is the remains of plants that sank in waterlogged soil. Over time, the plants turned to a rich soil called **peat**, before all the water and gas was squeezed out and all that was left was mostly **carbon** in the form of coal.

Petroleum and natural gas

Oil and gas is made from the remains of prehistoric marine organisms that were buried on the seabed and transformed by heat and pressure into a carbon-rich liquid and gas.

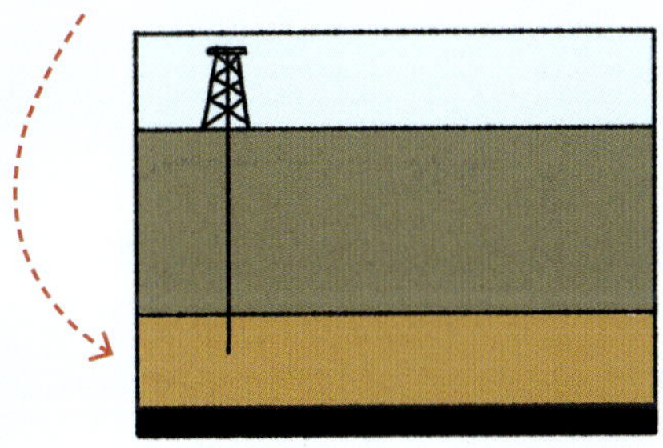

The burning of fossil fuels releases the gas carbon dioxide into the atmosphere. This traps in heat from the Sun and can warm up the planet above comfortable levels, which leads to extreme and unpredictable weather.

How to Pick Up a Billion Microbes
Scooter, could you add a little soil to this pot?

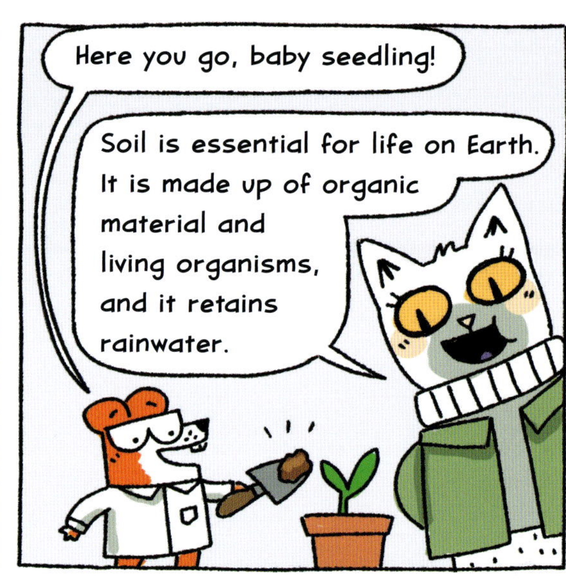
Here you go, baby seedling!
Soil is essential for life on Earth. It is made up of organic material and living organisms, and it retains rainwater.

Organisms in the soil remove harmful chemicals and recycle dead plants and animals, turning them into nutrients to feed new plants.
So soil is full of life?

Yes, and not just worms. There are tiny organisms called **MICROBES**, too small for us to see without a microscope.

There are about a billion microbes in every teaspoon of soil.

A billion?! I'm outnumbered!

All Change

(Changing Planet)

How to Move Mountains
Say cheese!
Gouda!

Hmm.
What's wrong, Scooter?

The mountain's in the way.
What do you expect?! We're hiking in the mountains.

I'd like it to be a little more to the left.
Well, if we hang around a few million years, it will move.
Mountains don't move!

Of course they do!
The mountains and all the continents are slowly moving under our feet.

No wonder I feel wobbly!
And it's time we got moving, too!

Earth's crust and the upper part of the mantle (the **lithosphere**) are divided into **tectonic plates** that slide over the molten part of the mantle called the **asthenosphere**.

Possibly due to rising heat from inside the Earth, the plates move about 2–20 cm (0.75–8 in) a year. Some are getting closer, some are moving apart.

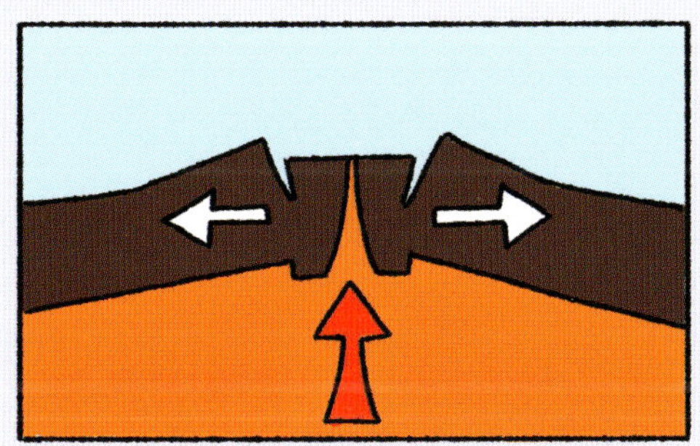

The place where plates move apart is called a **divergent boundary**. Underwater, magma can rise to fill the gap, forming a new crust. On land, the dividing plates can form a rift or valley.

The place where plates collide is called a **convergent boundary**. At this boundary, one of the plates may move above or below the other. On land, the crust can be pushed upward, forming mountain ranges.

The Andes mountains are getting higher every year as the oceanic Nazca plate is forced under the South American continental plate.

How to Make a Planet-sized Jigsaw
This Earth jigsaw puzzle is hard! So many pieces are plain blue!

That's because about 71 percent of the planet is covered in water!

You know Earth's crust is like a giant jigsaw puzzle?
Really?! Does it have this many pieces?

It has seven large pieces and about a dozen smaller pieces.
Where they meet, you may find high mountain ranges, deep ocean trenches, or violent volcanoes.

Are there any pieces missing?
No, why?

I've lost Australia.

The surface of Planet Earth is divided into seven large **tectonic plates** which surround the continents, along with several much smaller plates. Where they meet is where you'll find some of the most spectacular sights on the planet.

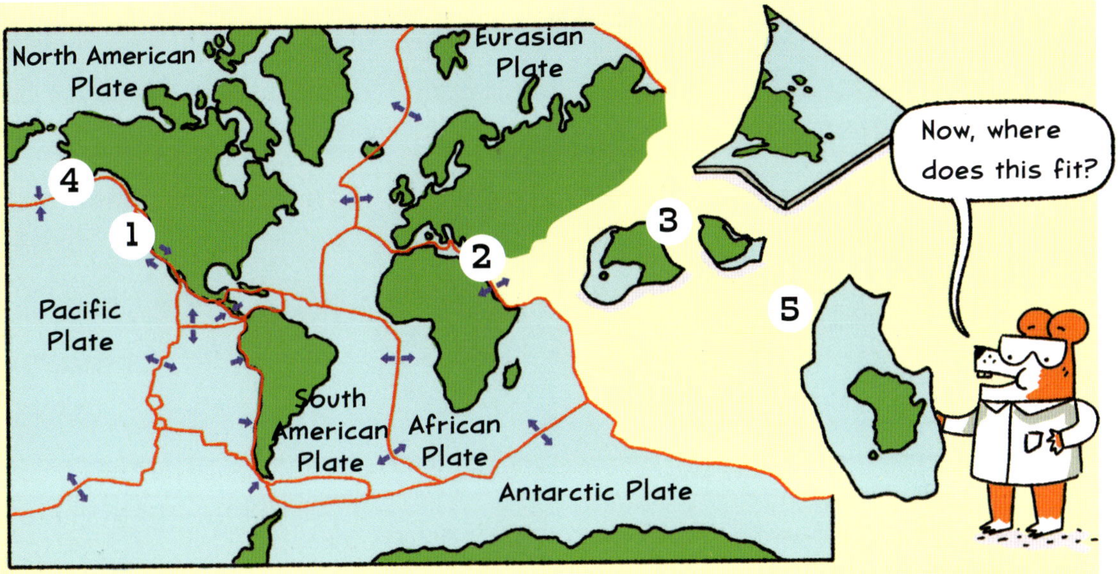

North American Plate
Eurasian Plate
Pacific Plate
South American Plate
African Plate
Antarctic Plate
Now, where does this fit?

1. The **San Andreas Fault** on the west coast of North America is the source of many earthquakes.
2. The **Red Sea** is getting wider as the African and Arabian plates move apart.
3. The **Himalayas** are rising where the Indian plate collides with Eurasia. 
4. The **Ring of Fire** along the edge of the Pacific Plate is dotted with two-thirds of the world's volcanoes.
5. The Pacific Plate moves under the Philippine Plate, and this is the lowest point on Earth, the **Mariana Trench**.

I've taped the world back together!
If only it was so simple!

The boundaries are where tectonic plates meet. When they collide or scrape against each other, earthquakes most often occur, or magma may erupt out of volcanoes.

Earth's Riches

Earth provides the perfect habitat for life, but it also supplies many **geological resources.** These include useful materials for construction and providing energy.

Metals

Gold and **copper** were among the first metals to be unearthed.

These were used mostly for decoration.

Other precious metals include **platinum** and **silver.** Alloys (combinations of metals) followed, such as **bronze** and **iron.** These were stronger than gold and were shaped into tools and weapons.

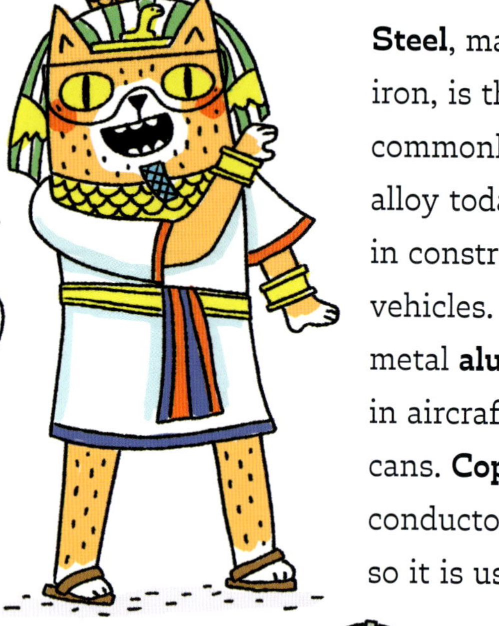

Steel, made from iron, is the most commonly used metal alloy today, especially in construction and vehicles. The light metal **aluminum** is used in aircraft and drinks cans. **Copper** is a good conductor of electricity, so it is used for wiring.

My helmet doesn't fit!

Minerals

Rocks have been dug from the earth and used for tools and building materials since prehistoric times when **flint** was gathered and sharpened for knives. Early buildings used clay, shaped and hardened in the sun to form bricks. Sand, clay, and many stones for building are extracted from the ground through deep pits called **quarries.**

Sand is used in the production of **concrete**, along with crushed stone (**aggregate**) and **limestone.**

Coal, gold, silver, and many gemstones are gathered through **mining** and digging shafts and tunnels into the ground.

Fossil fuels

Coal, oil, and gas are also extracted from the ground. Oil is also used in the production of plastics. Fossil fuels are **nonrenewable**, which means that once they are used up they cannot be replaced.

I'm doing an experiment, trying to break a rock with water.

I've poured water into a crack in the rock and now I'm freezing it to see if it will break.

Rocks on the Earth's surface can be worn away by **physical**, **chemical**, and biological weathering.

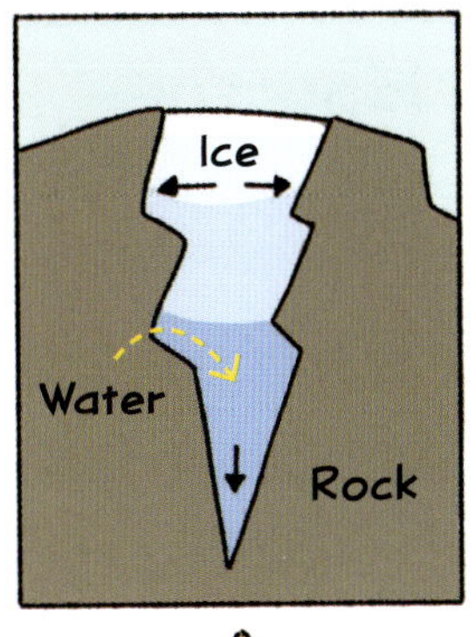

Physical weathering occurs with changes in temperature and pressure. Extremes of hot and cold can cause rocks to expand and contract. Water can get into cracks and open them wider when it freezes. Repeated changes in pressure as water freezes and thaws can fracture a rock.

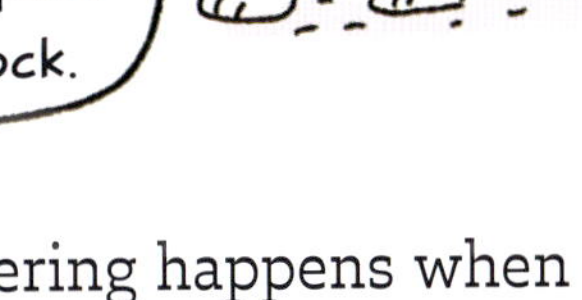

Chemical weathering happens when rain mixes with the atmospheric gas **carbon dioxide**. It becomes slightly acidic and can slowly dissolve rocks such as limestone.

Biological weathering is caused by animals and plants. If a seed falls into a crack in a rock, it may push the rock apart as it sprouts. Lichen is a plantlike organism which releases an acid that slowly dissolves minerals.

How to Carve a Canyon
Magnificent, isn't it! The result of six million years of erosion.
It's a long way down!

Come on, Scooter, let's hike to the bottom.
How long will it take?
The rest of the day.
What?!

Every step down we take we're traveling thousands of years back in geologic time.
The layers in the rocks mark different time periods and tell us what the climate was like long ago.

Will we find dinosaur bones?
Sorry, Scooter, the canyon rocks are much older than the dinosaurs, but billion-year-old marine fossils have been found.

Hours later ...
Here, near the bottom we can examine 1.8 billion-year-old rocks—that's a third the age of the Earth!
GASP!
All this is revealed thanks to a river wearing out the rock!

I don't think I can hike back. I'm worn out, too!

Erosion occurs when rocks are shaped by wind, water, and ice. Erosion can form impressive gorges and canyons.

Over time, the water in rivers and oceans can wear down riverbanks and cliffs. Rivers transport small rocks and **sediment** downstream. Most sediment is deposited on banks and where the river reaches the sea. Sediment provides nutrients for soil, benefiting farmers.

The **Grand Canyon** in the United States was carved by the Colorado River over a period of about six million years. It is 446 km (277 miles) long and is more than 1.6 km (1 mile) deep in places.

Water in the form of ice also carves rocks. **Glaciers** are large bodies of ice that move slowly down slopes or along valleys. The ice gathers lumps of rock as it moves, and these wear down the landscape that it moves over.

Wind can also shape the landscape through erosion, carrying away dust, sand, and soil. This is how sand dunes are formed in the deserts. Sand blown in the wind can wear down rocks through **wind abrasion**, to form interesting shapes.

How to
Lose a Hill
What a lovely day for a walk along the ridge.

Oh! Where did the hill go?

Are we lost?
No, but the hill and path have gone.

How is that possible? Was it aliens?
The warning sign says there's been a landslide.

Look!
The hill moved downhill!
It could be heavy rainfall, frost, even an earthquake that caused it.
It's lucky we weren't here when it happened.

Let's take a detour.
Yes. I like the ground to stay put!

Hillsides and cliffs are usually stable but they can be at risk of collapse after extreme weather, underground movements, or as the result of human activity. Then, **landslides** or **landslips** may result.

Tension cracks

Scarp

Tilted blocks

Toe

Tension cracks are a sign of a possible landslide as a block of ground begins to move. When it drops, a vertical face called a **scarp** is revealed. The debris at the front of the landslide is called the **toe**.

Earthquakes or volcanic eruptions can loosen the ground. Heavy rain soaking the soil or roadbuilding, mining, and deforestation may make a landslide possible.

The ground may slide downhill in one large block or break up and pour down a slope like a sea of mud. The slide may be slow or dangerously fast on the steepest slopes and may cause great damage to property in its way.

How to Make a Shake
Where do you want these pots, Dr. Ringtail?
Just over ...

Why is everything shaking?
RRUMBLE!
That's odd. We're not in an earthquake zone.

An EARTHQUAKE?! Hide under the table!
RRUMBLE!

It's stopped.
We should check on Katzenstein.

RRUMBLE!
It's happening again!
Hey, guys! Check out my new INDUSTRIAL MILKSHAKE MAKER! It's really powerful.

Anyone for a shake?

When large volumes of rock in Earth's upper layers are divided, this is called a **fault**. Faults are most often found where tectonic plates meet.

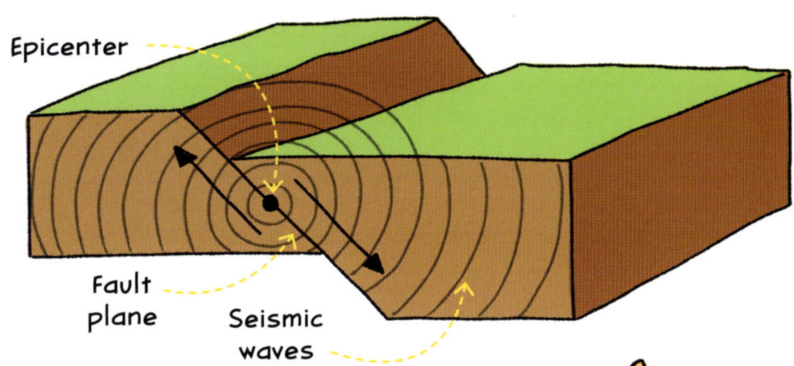

If there is a sudden fault movement with the rocks sliding in different directions, this can cause ground vibrations or **seismic waves** that are felt as mild **tremors** or powerful **earthquakes**. The vibrations come from a point called the **epicenter**.

Why are you shaking, Scooter?

I'm worried about earthquakes.

The most powerful earthquake ever recorded measured 9.5 and happened in Chile in 1960.

The strength of an earthquake is measured on the **Richter scale**, where 1 is a small movement, 5 is a medium quake that can cause slight damage to buildings, and 10 is a disaster.

Richter scale

9
8
7
6
5
4
3
2
1

Countries where earthquakes are common have strict building regulations to prevent collapse, with strong, flexible materials used and shock absorbers fitted, so vibrations do not seriously damage a structure.

But major earthquakes are rare.

How to Drink Dinosaur Pee
What did the dinosaurs drink, Professor?
They drank the same water that you're drinking, Scooter.

In fact, the water you're drinking was once dinosaur pee.
SPLURT!

What?!
It's perfectly fine, Scooter. Earth's water has been recycled for billions of years.
Follow me ...

Water is essential for life.
There is about 1.4 billion cubic km (333 million cubic miles) of it on the Earth.
That's a lot of bottles full!

Most of the water is in the oceans, with a small percent as ice in glaciers and ice sheets.
Much of it goes on a journey called the WATER CYCLE, which cleans it.

When water is warmed up by the Sun, it evaporates—turning to a gas or vapor of pure water.
Going up!

We have a limited amount of water to share on Earth. We should keep it clean and be grateful for it!

And thank you, dinosaurs!

QUACK!

How to Make an Impact

Millions of **meteoroids** enter Earth's atmosphere every day. Most come from the Asteroid Belt between Mars and Jupiter and arrive as grains of dust that burn up due to **friction** with the air. But, some are large enough to survive entry and hit the ground as **meteorites**. The largest can leave craters on the ground where they hit. These impacts are very rare.

Meteor Crater in Arizona, USA, is 1.2 km (0.75 miles) across, the result of an impact from a 50 m (150 ft)-wide meteorite about 50,000 years ago.

How to Escape a Wall of Water
Not swimming, Scooter?
The waves look too high.
You don't need to worry about **TSUNAMIS** here, Scooter.

Tsunamis?
Tsunamis are huge waves usually caused by earthquakes.

They may appear like walls of water and can travel up to 50 km/h (30 mph), with waves 30 m (100 ft) high.
That's higher than a house! How can you swim in that?

You don't.
If you're in a tsunami risk area and see the water moving away from the coast, that's a first sign of a tsunami.

You should hurry along the evacuation route to higher ground.
This talk of tsunamis makes me feel like ice cream.
How come?

There's an ice-cream store on higher ground.

Land Ahoy!

(Land)

How to Blow Your Top
Here we are on the **RING OF FIRE**, Scooter!
What's the Ring of Fire?

The Ring of Fire is a highly active belt of volcanoes around the edge of the Pacific Ocean plate.
BOOM!
Whoa!

Why are we here?
Because we're fearless scientists, going to extremes to find out how the Earth works.

Don't worry, Scooter. We're a safe distance away from the eruptions.
Earthquakes, however ...

RRUMBLE!
Oh dear. Is that the sound of an earthquake?

RRUMBLE!
That's my stomach rumbling.

Volcanoes are vents on Earth's surface where molten rock called **magma** escapes from below the crust. When magma reaches the surface, it is called **lava**. Most volcanoes appear where **tectonic plates** meet, and they can be found on land and underwater.

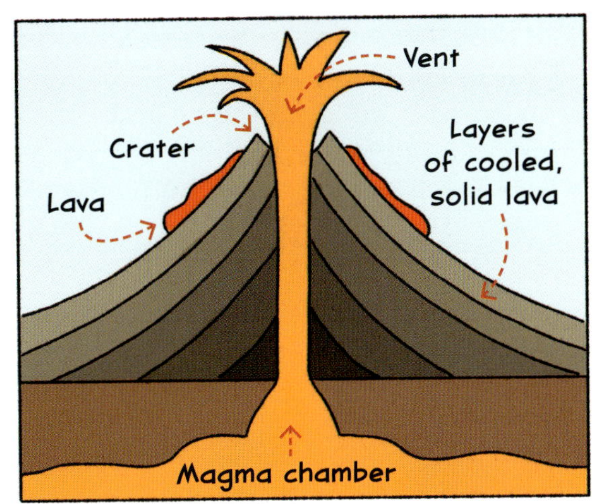

The cone shape of a volcano is the result of many layers of lava pouring out of a vent from beneath Earth's crust, then cooling and turning into solid rock. As well as lava, volcanoes can release a dangerous **pyroclastic flow**, made up of large amounts of ash, gas, and chunks of hot rock.

If all the magma in a **magma chamber** under the volcano is released, the volcano may collapse and leave behind a crater called a **caldera**. When volcanoes no longer show signs of erupting, they are called **dormant**. Those that are not expected to erupt again are called **extinct**.

How to
Surf a Volcano
Puff! Pant!
Nearly there, Scooter!

Gasp! Why are we walking up an active volcano?
Trudging through ash is like walking up a sand dune!

And why are you carrying a board?
You'll see!

Why do we need helmets and kneepads?
Just in case ...

We're not going into the volcano, are we?!

No, just down it!
Waaaaaugh!

There are about 1,500 active volcanoes on Earth, and between 50 and 70 of them erupt every year. Active volcanoes near towns and cities are regularly monitored. Many receive regular visitors, not just volcano experts known as **vulcanologists**, but extreme sports fans.

Climbing up a volcano over loose volcanic stones and ash can be hard work, but getting down can be fun, if risky. The best way to get down may be sliding.

Enthusiasts have turned this into a sport called **volcano boarding**, something like snowboarding. A special board is used, with a slippery bottom surface. Boarders hold on to it with a rope.

The most popular sites for the sport are Cerro Negro in Nicaragua and Mount Bromo in Indonesia. These volcanoes are active and release fresh volcanic ash regularly, which provides a smooth surface.

VOLCANO BOARDING CAN BE DANGEROUS AND SHOULD ONLY BE DONE BY ADULTS WITH AN EXPERIENCED GUIDE.

How to Climb Everest
Phew! Made it!
It's not every day we get to stand on top of the world!

What do you mean "top of the world"?
MOUNT EVEREST, the world's highest mountain.

Scooter, we're only at the start of the trail.
THAT'S Mount Everest!

It will take us two weeks to reach base camp.
Two weeks?!

Everest and the Himalayas were raised from the seabed as the Indian tectonic plate collided with the Eurasian Plate.
So Everest was once at the bottom of the sea?!
Yes, about 50 million years ago.

It's made of marine limestone, and you can find fossils of prehistoric sea creatures near the top.

Everest is 8,848 m (29,032 ft) above sea level and still growing.
We'd better hurry to climb it before it gets bigger!
It's only growing by about 1 cm (0.4 in) every 10 years!

Puff! Pant! Why am I so out of breath?
That's because there's less oxygen the higher we go. Most Everest climbers carry an oxygen supply.

We'll need local guides called sherpas to lead us up the mountain with ropes and ladders.
It sounds dangerous!

It is. There's the thin air, freezing temperature, chance of storms, avalanches, and the Death Zone ...
Death Zone?!

That's the toughest part near the summit. About 300 people have died trying the climb.
Gulp!

All of a sudden, I don't feel I need to be the first guinea pig on Everest.
Good. Let's make *looking* at the Himalayas the high point of our day.

How to Be Boiled

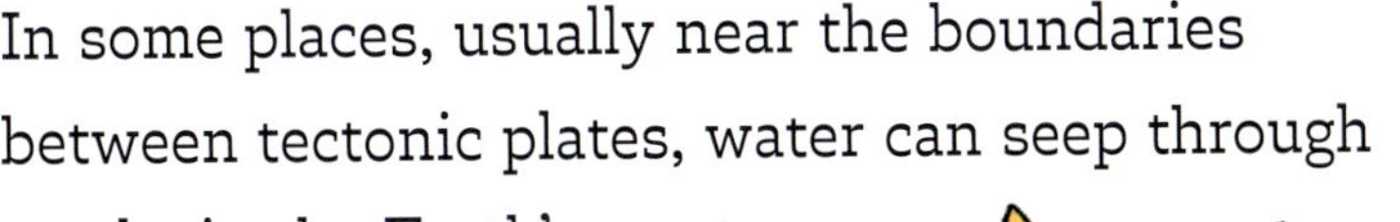

In some places, usually near the boundaries between tectonic plates, water can seep through cracks in the Earth's crust. Deep underground, the water is **superheated** by hot rocks before returning to the surface to form **hot springs**.

While a few hot springs are comfortable for bathing in, many are boiling hot and can be 174 °C (345 °F) in the deepest parts. Under the oceans, water can emerge from Earth's crust at temperatures up to 400 °C (750 °F)—as hot as Mercury, the closest planet to the Sun. Despite high temperatures, some microorganisms, like **bacteria**, can survive in hot springs.

Hot springs often contain **minerals** dissolved from the rocks the water passed on its way to the surface. Some of these minerals are thought to offer health benefits.

How to Let Off Steam

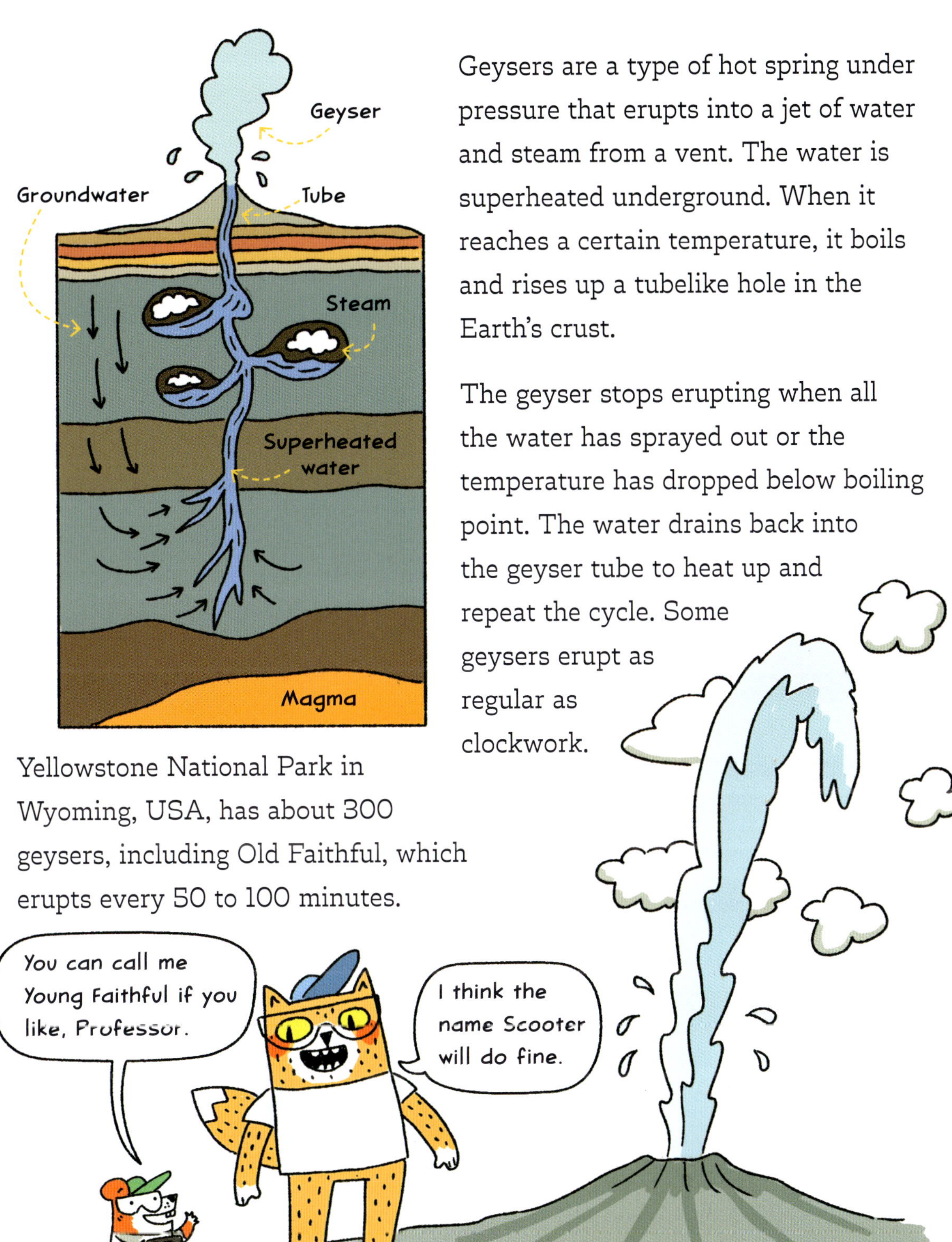

Geysers are a type of hot spring under pressure that erupts into a jet of water and steam from a vent. The water is superheated underground. When it reaches a certain temperature, it boils and rises up a tubelike hole in the Earth's crust.

The geyser stops erupting when all the water has sprayed out or the temperature has dropped below boiling point. The water drains back into the geyser tube to heat up and repeat the cycle. Some geysers erupt as regular as clockwork.

Yellowstone National Park in Wyoming, USA, has about 300 geysers, including Old Faithful, which erupts every 50 to 100 minutes.

Other places to find geysers include Chile, Iceland, and New Zealand.

Geysers have also been located on moons in the Solar System.

How to Take an Eggy Shower

Geothermal energy is energy stored as heat underground. Deep below, the Earth is very hot from the time of its formation and from the **radioactive decay** of elements in the crust. This heats water that seeps through the rocks and produces hot springs.

Cooling towers
Electrical energy
Turbine and generator
Steam
Injection well
Hot water
Magma

This hot water can be used for heating homes and buildings. Steam and hot water can also be used to power turbines that generate electricity.

Geothermal energy is used all over the world and is a major energy source in countries with a lot of volcanic activity, such as El Salvador, the Philippines, and Iceland.

The hot springs that provide geothermic energy in Iceland also contain lots of dissolved minerals, including **hydrogen sulfide.** It's perfectly safe, and you don't end up smelling eggy after a shower.

How to Ride the Rapids
I've never been **WHITE WATER RAFTING** before, Professor. It's quite relaxing.
Well, we haven't hit the **RAPIDS** yet.

Rapids?
That's where the gradient of the river drops, and the water moves faster.
We'll need to paddle fast, to avoid the rocks.

That doesn't sound so relaxing.
It's supposed to be exciting, Scooter.
Each rapid has a number rating for how dangerous it is.

Whoa!
That was class 3, not too hard.

Waugh!
I've got you, Scooter.
This is level 4.
How high does it go?

There's a level 10 ahead that might be tricky.

Rivers form as **fresh water** from rain, snow, and **glaciers** finds a path through the land to reach the sea or a lake. Powered by gravity, rivers have worn their way through rocks to shape canyons and valleys.

Rivers begin with a **source**. This may be a spring where rainwater gathers or ice melts from a glacier. The water drains downhill in a small stream. Several streams, or **tributaries**, may merge into a large river at a point called a **confluence**. Where there is a sudden drop in height, you might find **rapids** or **waterfalls**. Finally, the river reaches the sea or a lake at its **mouth**.

Some rivers end with a **delta**, where the river breaks into many small channels and new islands are created from the sediment carried downstream. Every year, about 20 billion metric tons (22 billion tons) of land surface or **sediment** is washed away to the oceans by rivers.

How to Sail Up High
Puff! Pant!
Rowing is hard work! Could you help?

I've already got an important job to do—guiding.
Head east!

I need to catch my breath.
You may be affected by the ALTITUDE.
The air is thinner here.

I'm thinner, too. I haven't had a snack since we set off!
I meant that there's less oxygen at this height.

Lake Titicaca is 3,812 m (12,526 ft) above sea level.

No wonder I'm tired! I've been rowing uphill!

Lakes form in depressions in the ground, often the result of **glaciers**. They may be the source of a river, like Lake Victoria, the source of the Nile, or the end point for a stream. Most contain fresh water.

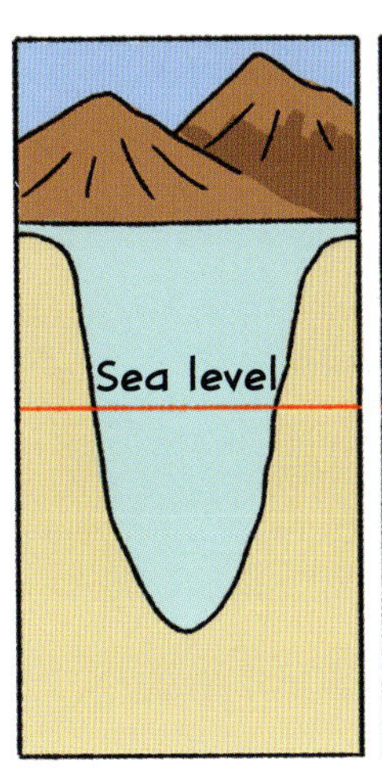

Lake Tanganika 1,471 m (4,800 ft)

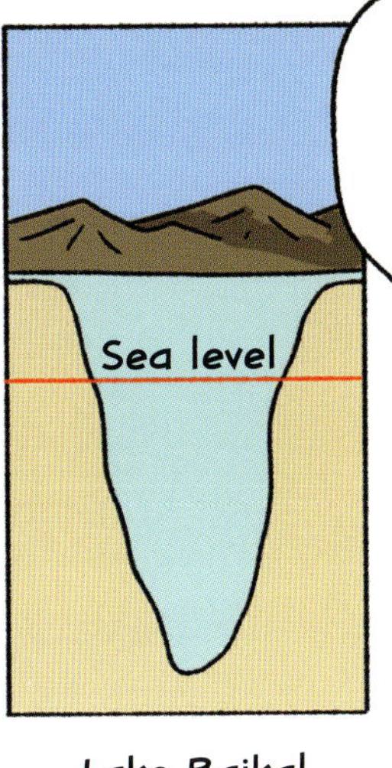

Lake Baikal 1,741 m (5,716 ft)

These lakes are the oldest in the world ... and the deepest!

Some lakes are formed in volcanic craters or collapsed caves. Siberia's **Lake Baikal** and Africa's **Lake Tanganika** appeared where fault lines in the Earth's crust divided and filled with water.

The **Caspian Sea**, in Eastern Europe, is the world's largest lake, with a surface area of 371,000 km^2 (143,243 sq mi). It was once part of a prehistoric ocean before being cut off. Its water is salty.

Lake Titicaca, between Peru and Bolivia in South America, is the highest lake that can be sailed across. It is 3.8 km (2.4 miles) above sea level, higher than the top of Mount Fuji in Japan!

Lake Titicaca 3.8 km (2.4 miles) high

The people that live around Lake Titicaca collect reeds from the banks and use them to build boats and houses.

Mount Fuji 3.78 km (2.35 miles) high

How to Grow a Grotto
This cave took millions of years to grow to this size.
Wow! It's like a fairy grotto!

Look above at the stalactites growing from the roof.

And stalagmites growing from the ground.
Some of them are funny shapes.

I'll name this one Stumpy.
I'll name this Test Tube.
Boring name!

OK, I'll name this one Pagoda.
I'll name this Norman.
Why Norman?

My friend Norman wears a pointed hat.

Caves are underground spaces in the rocks large enough for a person to enter. Most are formed in limestone where slightly acidic rain and groundwater has seeped in through cracks and dissolved some of the rocks over time.

As water slowly drips through the limestone, it can leave a build-up of **calcium carbonate** in the form of **stalactites**, **stalagmites**, and **columns**.

Stalactites are icicle-like shapes that descend from the cave roof. Water dripping from stalactites can form conelike **stalagmites** on the ground.When stalactites and stalagmites eventually meet, they can form **columns**.

Some cave systems have passages that extend for miles. **Mammoth Cave** in Kentucky, USA, has 676 km (420 miles) of explored underground passageways. Other caves are underwater and popular with scuba divers. Another type of cave is a **lava tube**, where hot lava once flowed.

While some caves are paved and lit for visitors, others can be dangerous places, with tight squeezes, streams, pits, and the chance of getting lost. These caves should only be explored with the help of an experienced guide.

How to Cross a Crevasse
Here we are! Are you ready to cross the **GLACIER**, Scooter?
It looks very slippery.

That's why we need to wear **CRAMPONS**.
The spikes should keep us from slipping on the ice.

Watch out for **CREVASSES**!
What are they?
Deep cracks in the ice. If you fall into one, it could be 100 years before you're found at the bottom of the glacier where the ice melts.
100 years?

Scooter, welcome!
You've been frozen in the ice for a century!
Wow, I'm in the future!

Yes, and now we guinea pigs are ruling the Earth!
Hooray!

Scooter!
Stop daydreaming. We can use this ladder to cross the crevasse.

Glaciers are moving bodies of ice made by compressed and frozen snow. Most glaciers are found over cold mountain slopes. The ice in glaciers holds about 70 percent of all the world's fresh water.

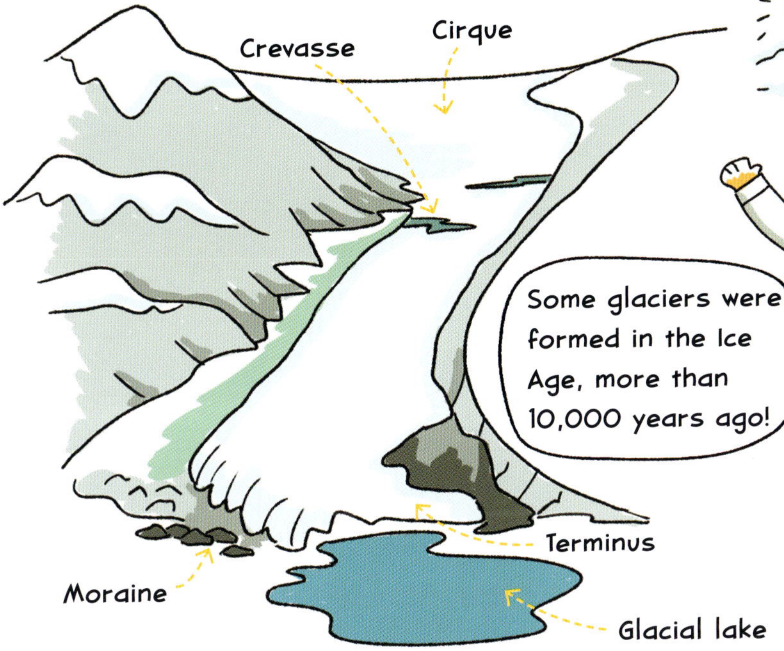

The top of a glacier is usually found in a bowl-shaped area called a **cirque**, where fresh snow may fall to refresh the glacier. Below this, the ice descends and may crack into **crevasses**. The pull of gravity moves the glacier downhill.

The glacier ends at its **terminus**, where it melts and deposits debris collected on its path. The rocks left behind by a glacier are called a **moraine**. Here, the ice slowly melts away. Some glaciers end with a lake. Some reach the sea, where large pieces break off with a crash.

The Biosphere

Life has adapted to live all over the planet, on land and in the sea. It inhabits a thin layer of the Earth called the **biosphere**, about 20 km (12 miles) deep, from the top of the highest mountain to the bottom of the deepest ocean trench.

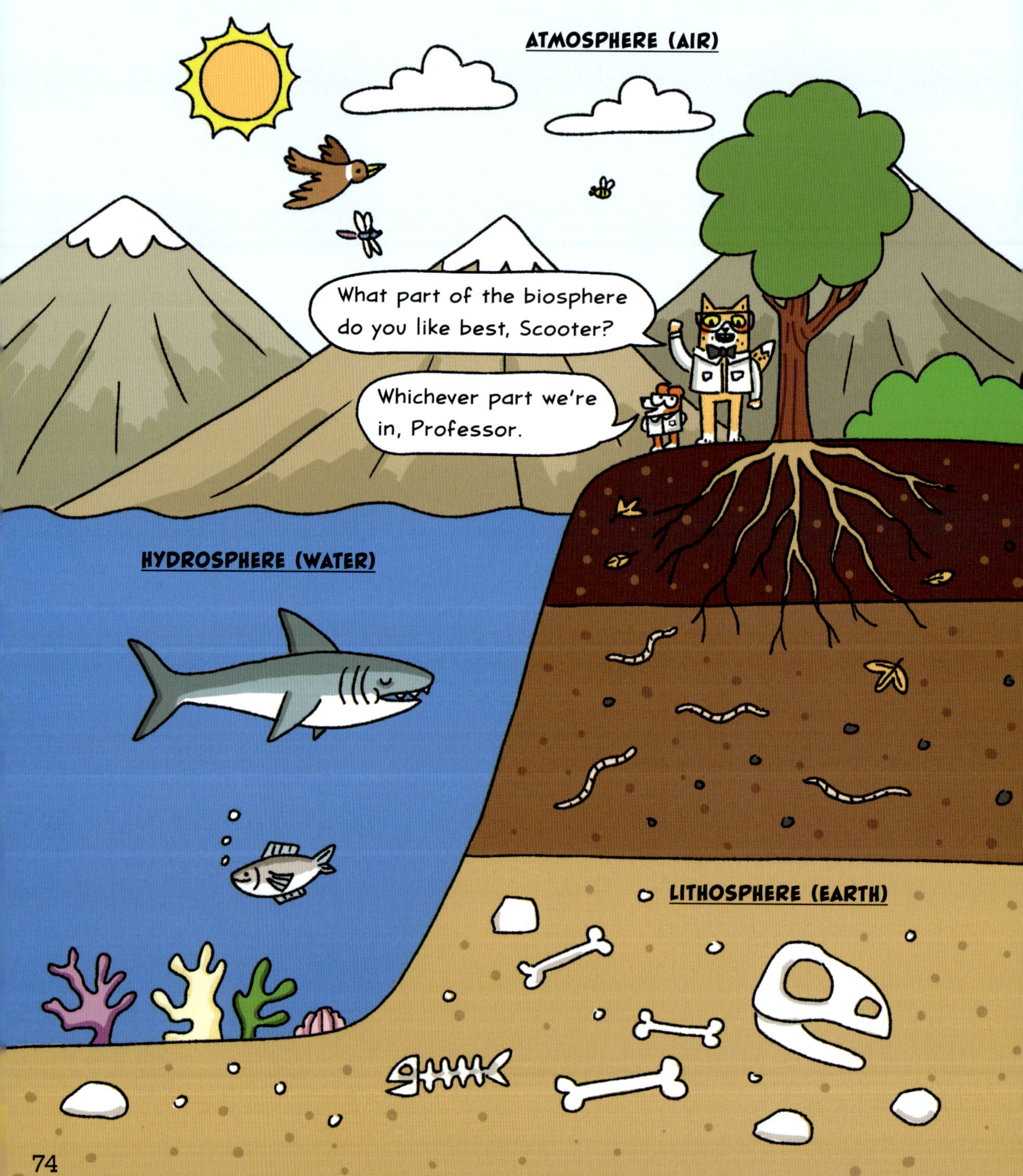

Almost all life depends on sunlight to survive. Plants and algae use sunlight to produce the sugars they need to grow and they can then add oxygen to the **atmosphere** (air). In turn, plants are eaten by animals, giving them the energy to survive, and dead plants and animals decompose and return nutrients to the **lithosphere** (earth) and **hydrosphere** (water). This circle of food and energy sustains life on the planet.

The biosphere is made up of different **ecosystems**, smaller circles of life where plants, animals, and other organisms exist in an environment that provides good shelter and weather conditions.

Most life exists in a small band from 500 m (1,640 ft) underwater to 6 km (3.75 miles) above sea level, with many species found in and around rain forests and coral reefs. But life can be found in the most extreme environments. Fish live as deep as 8.4 km (5.2 miles) in the oceans, while geese have been seen flying 5.4 km (3.6 miles) above the height of the Himalayan mountains.

How to Avoid Rain
Another wet and miserable day. Can we go somewhere dry?
How about a desert?
Sounds good!

Some time later ...
Welcome to the world's largest desert, Scooter.
It's freezing! And where's all the sand?

This is the Antarctic Desert. There's no sand but lots of snow and ice.
Deserts are places with very little rain, and Antarctica only gets a few inches a year.
Can we go somewhere warmer?

Even later ...
How about the Sahara, the largest sandy desert in the world?
I hope you remembered to bring some water ...

Even better, I've got some ice from Antarctica in my pocket ...

Oh ...

Deserts are the driest places on the planet where less than 25 cm (10 in) of rain falls each year. They cover 20 percent of the Earth's land.

The African **Sahara** is the largest hot desert in the world. Temperatures reach up to 50 °C (122 °F) in the daytime. Dust and sand gets blown into great dunes by the wind. Sometimes the dust and sand is launched into the air as a **sandstorm** more than 1.6 km (1 mile) high which can last for hours.

Without rain, few plants and animals can survive. When it does rain in hot deserts, the rainwater **evaporates** quickly due to the heat. Rare areas of fresh water do exist, however, with water from underground wells forming **oases**.

Desert plants have few leaves and are often spiky, like cacti, to keep them from being eaten. They may stay **dormant** for months, waiting for rain. Desert animals are often **nocturnal**, living in burrows, then coming out to hunt at night when it is cooler.

The world's largest desert is a cold one. The **Antarctic Desert** covers the whole continent. Around the South Pole, it is too cold for water vapor to form clouds, so there is very little rain.

How to Live in the Canopy
Scooter? Scooter?

Up here!
What are you doing in the tree?

I've found my perfect habitat, the **FOREST CANOPY**.
I didn't think you liked heights.

I don't. That's why I've tied myself to a branch with elastic rope.
And there is fruit on the tree that I can feed on ...

Whoops!

Waugh!!
BOING!
BOING!
Now you can enjoy all the tree levels at once!

Tropical rain forests are one of the most important environments on Earth. They are home to more than half of the world's plant and animal species. The plants help add the oxygen to the air that we need to breathe. These forests are moist and receive a lot of rain.

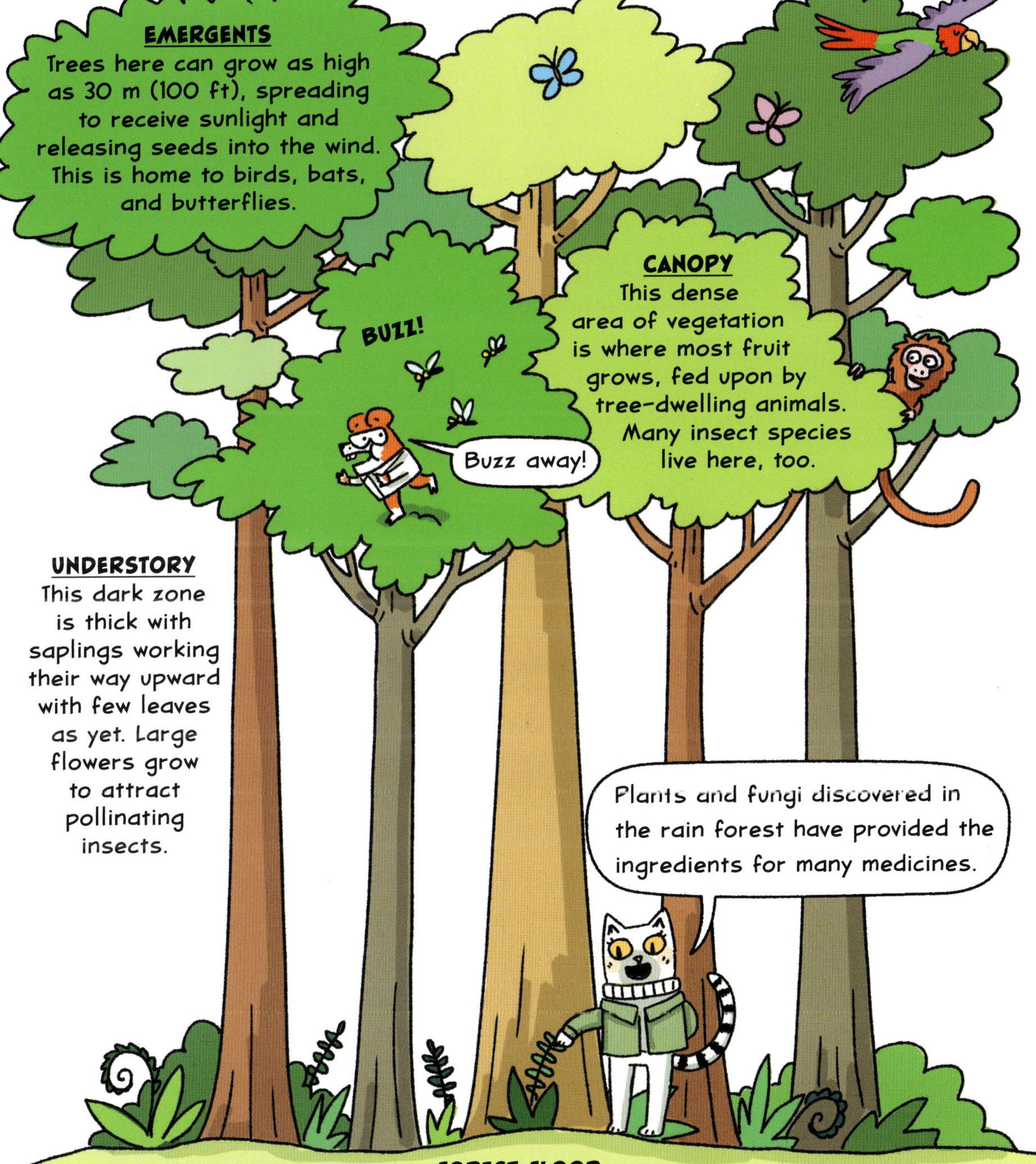

How to Run a Farm
I've dreamed of owning my own farm.
You're joining a proud tradition. Agriculture provides work for 40 percent of the world's population.

Almost half of the world's habitable land is used for agriculture.
Is it hard work?

It is, but it's rewarding.
First, you'll need to dig your land well.

Then, plant your crop in rows, keep it watered and fed with nutrients, before harvesting.

Have you thought about what you'd like to grow?
Yes, birds.
You can't grow birds!

So what is this BIRDSEED for?!

Off the Deep End

(Ocean)

How to Plunge the Depths
Here we are, Scooter. Are you ready to dive the MARIANA TRENCH?
SLURP!
It just looks like normal sea to me.

The Mariana Trench is the LOWEST POINT on Earth!
Will we have enough air in our scuba tanks?

We can't dive that deep in WET SUITS!
We'll need to use the SUBMERSIBLE.

It's a SQUEEZE in here, even for me.
You'll feel more of a squeeze if you go outside.

The pressure near the bottom is over a thousand times the pressure on the surface.
What's that mean?

Gulp! That really would be a LOW POINT!
KRINCH!

The **Mariana Trench** is the lowest point on Earth. It is found in the western Pacific Ocean, near the Mariana Islands where the Pacific tectonic plate pushes under the Philippine plate.

2 km (1.2 miles)

Mariana Trench 10,984 m (36,037 ft)

Mount Everest 8,849 m (29,032 ft)

If Mount Everest was dropped in it, there would still be 2 km (1.2 miles) of sea above it.

And there would be a **BIG SPLASH** too!

The bottom of the trench is in complete darkness. The pressure from all the water above is over a thousand times the atmospheric pressure (the pressure in the air around you) felt at sea level. Divers need to travel in a superstrong submersible to explore the depths, and it can take over an hour to reach the bottom.

Incredibly, there are fish, shrimp, and plankton living in the lower parts of the trench. Some of them make their own light to send signals and find food.

How to Survive Without Sunlight
When you said we were going to the Tropics, I expected a beach vacation.
There is a beach but it's about two kilometers above us.

I want to go somewhere warm.
That's where we're headed!
Hooray!

It's a HYDROTHERMAL VENT.
Oh.

Most plants and animals need energy from the Sun to grow ...
... But here on the dark, deep seabed, they feed on minerals released by underwater hot jets.

I don't think I could live without the Sun.
Why's that?

I look too good in shades.

Hydrothermal vents are areas on the seabed where water, superheated by magma inside the Earth, is released through cracks in the oceanic crust, like hot springs on land.

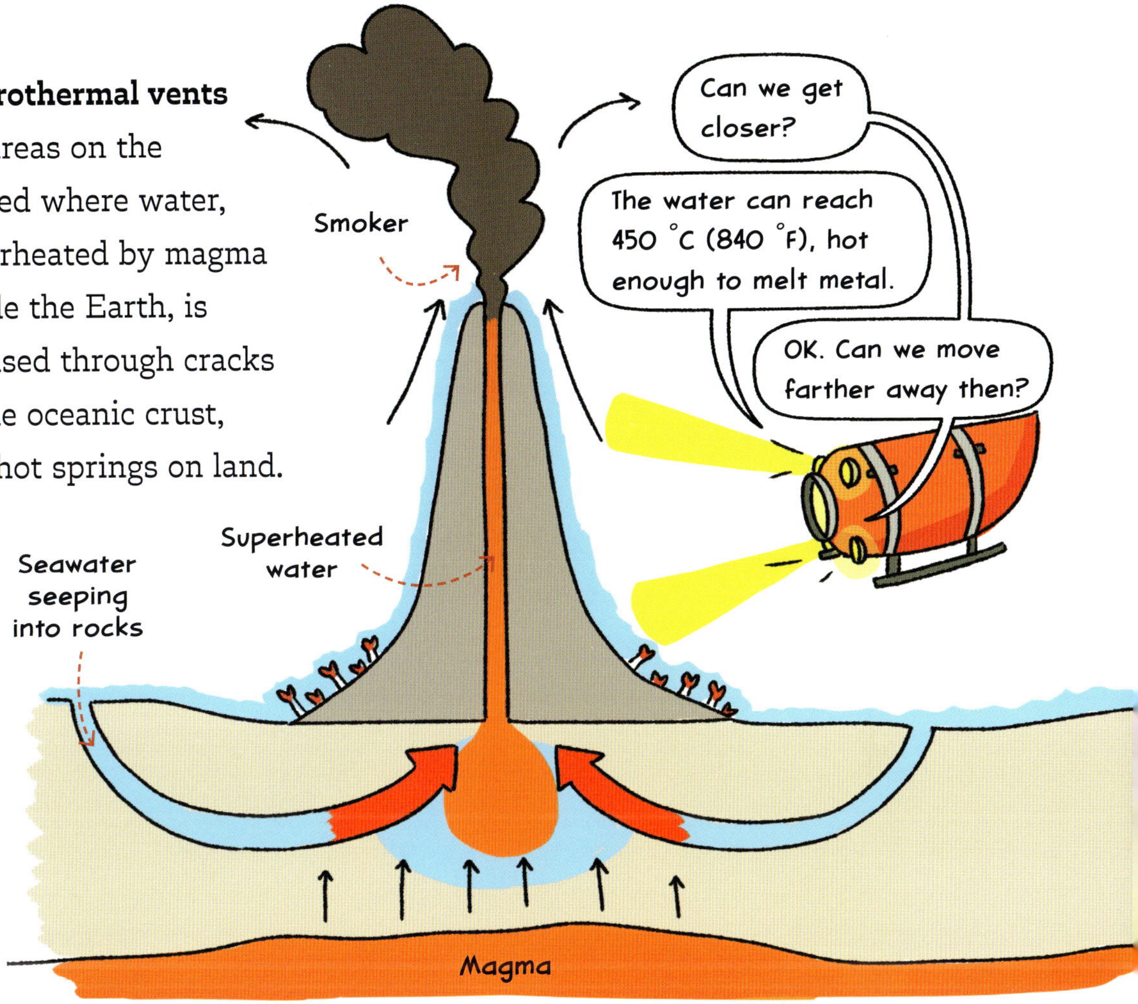

Smoker

Can we get closer?

The water can reach 450 °C (840 °F), hot enough to melt metal.

OK. Can we move farther away then?

Superheated water

Seawater seeping into rocks

Magma

Along with the boiling water are many minerals that have dissolved from rocks. These cool down when in contact with seawater and create clouds, like chimney smoke, which is why they are called **smokers**.

Some of the minerals in these clouds build chimneys around the vents up to 55 m (180 ft) tall. Some are taken in by **bacteria.** The bacteria become food for creatures that live around the hydrothermal vents.

Animals you can find around hydrothermal vents include mussels, shrimp, white yeti crabs, and giant tube worms.

That Sinking Feeling

The ocean is divided into five depth zones depending on how much sunlight reaches down. From the top to the bottom, they are the **sunlight zone**, **twilight zone**, **midnight zone**, **abyssal zone**, and the **trenches**.

ABYSSAL ZONE (ABYSSOPELAGIC)
This zone is pitch-black and near freezing. Very little of this region has been explored. Few animals are thought to live here.

SUNLIGHT ZONE (EPIPELAGIC)

This zone receives the most light. This is where you'll find coral reefs and 90 percent of all marine life, including sharks, tuna, and dolphins.

TWILIGHT ZONE (MESOPELAGIC)

This zone is darker. It is home to jellyfish and small shrimp called krill that feed on sinking animal remains known as **MARINE SNOW**.

200 m (650 ft)

Fish here have larger eyes to see better in the dim light.

1,000 m (3,280 ft)

MIDNIGHT ZONE (BATHYPELAGIC)

To find food in this chilly zone some sea creatures use **BIOLUMINESCENCE**, creating their own light using chemicals in their body.

4,000 m (13,000 ft)

6,500 m (21,000 ft)

Creatures can survive the huge pressure in the deep because their bodies are made of mostly water under the same pressure.

TRENCHES (HADOPELAGIC)

The trenches, such as the Mariana Trench (page 83), go even deeper. Despite the enormous water pressure, some fish and plankton survive here.

11,000 m (36,000 ft)

How to Move the Sea

Tides are mostly caused by the **gravitational pull** of the Moon on Earth. The pull causes the Earth and its water to bulge slightly with a **tidal force**. This bulge causes a **high tide**, when the water moves closer to a shore.

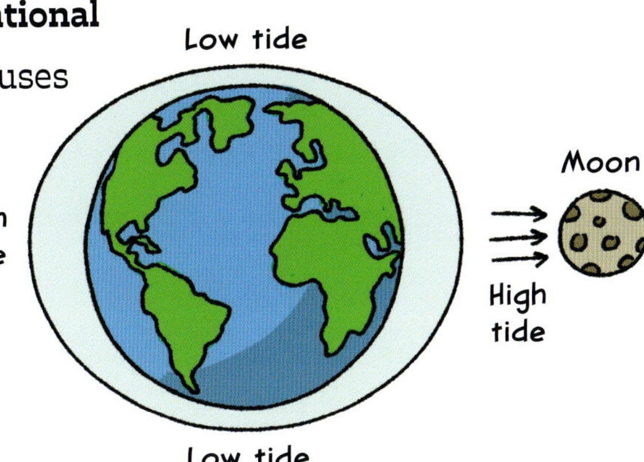

As the Earth spins, the gravitational pull of the Moon affects different parts of the planet. Most coastlines on Earth experience two high tides and two low tides in a day.

The difference between high and low tides is also affected by the depth of the ocean and land getting in the way. The average difference in height between high and low tide (**tidal range**) is 1 m (3.3 ft), but in some places it can be 10 times this amount!

When the Sun and Moon are in line every 14 days, around the time of a new or full moon, the gravitational pull of both of them on Earth causes more extreme tides, called **spring tides**. When they pull in opposite directions, the tides are smaller. These are known as **neap tides**.

How to Escape a Whirlpool
The current feels strong. It's hard to paddle.
Try paddling in a straight line, Scooter.

I'm going in circles.
I'm caught in a **WHIRLPOOL**!

Don't panic, Scooter. It's just an area where opposing water **CURRENTS** are meeting.
Follow the direction of its spin, and use it to launch yourself past.

It's no good, I'm just going in a circle.
Save yourself. I'm doomed!

Hold on ... there's no whirlpool ...

You're going around because you're just paddling right!

Air above land is heated by the Sun faster than the air above water. As warm air rises, it is replaced by cool air. This air movement is **wind**. The wind creates surface **ocean currents** that move heat across the globe, along with nutrients and the eggs of marine species.

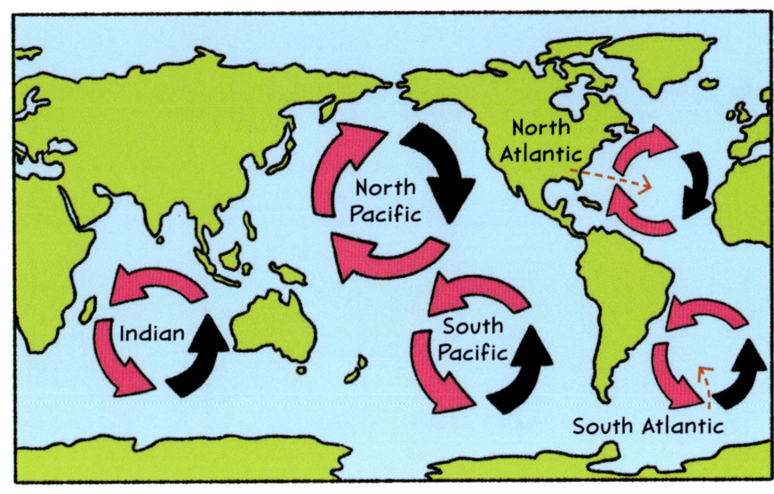

The currents move in loops called **gyres**. There are five major gyres rotating across the oceans.

The Coriolis effect deflects the path of wind and water currents, so that they move in different directions. In the northern hemisphere, the gyres turn clockwise. In the south, they move counterclockwise.

There are currents below the ocean surface, too. These deep ocean currents are caused by differences in water temperature and saltiness. Cold, salty water is more dense than warm, less salty water, so it sinks. This is called **downwelling**. Water moving upward (**upwelling**) brings nutrients with it that help feed fish and marine mammals.

How to Avoid an Iceberg
Here we are by the Greenland ice sheet, Scooter. What do you think?
It's, um, cool.

KERASHH!
Waugh!
Wow! A block of ice has broken free!

Hold on! There will be a big wave.
Whoa!

Now we have a new iceberg.
It doesn't look very big.
You're only looking at a tiny part of it. Most is underwater.

Look! Here's a really tiny iceberg!

Whoa!

Icebergs are large chunks of ice that have broken away from a **glacier** (page 73) or **ice shelf** (a thick, mass of ice) to float in open water.

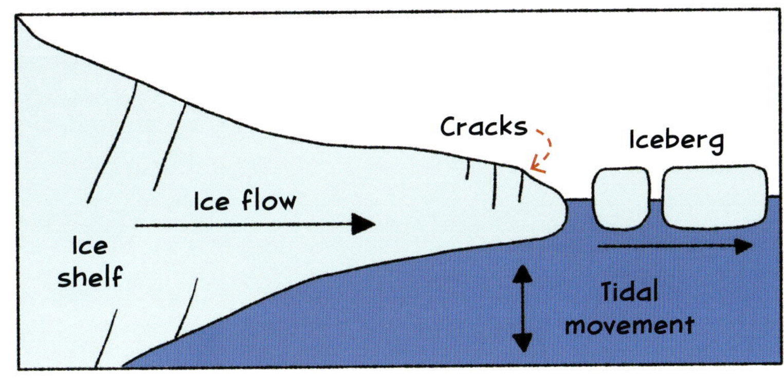

They may break away due to tidal movement below the ice. The movement causes the ice to crack. Eventually, the crack becomes so deep that a block of ice may break free.

The largest recorded iceberg, sighted in the South Pacific Ocean in 1956, was 335 x 97 km (208 x 60 mi) in size.

That's bigger than Belgium!

What is seen above water is just the top. About 90 percent of the iceberg is underwater, so ships need to keep far away.

Due to climate change, large ice shelves are melting and breaking into icebergs more often. As this ice melts, it could cause sea levels to rise and affect ocean currents.

Ice reflects sunlight, too, so the less ice there is on Earth, the warmer the planet gets.

90% of sunlight reflected by ice

6% reflected by water

Top of the World
Puff! Pant!
Keep up, Scooter!
The North Pole awaits.

It's freezing!
Of course, it is! We're in the Arctic, where temperatures can drop to −50 °C (−58 °F).

Scooter?

Use your hiking poles to probe the snow, Scooter, so you know it's hard enough to walk on.
Huff!

Do you know there's no land below us, only a thick layer of snow and ice?
You mean I could have fallen through into the sea?!

I would be more worried about polar bears.
Wha?!

The geographic North Pole is the northernmost point on Earth.

The magnetic North Pole depends on Earth's magnetic field. It moves around and can be hundreds of miles from the top of the world.

How to Gather Garbage
Thank you for helping me pick up litter from the beach, Scooter.
I'm happy to.

Is that a plastic bag?
Careful! It's a JELLYFISH. It might still sting.
Oooh!

It's a shame that so much litter ends up on the beach.
This is just what the tide brings in.

In the ocean, there are large areas where plastic waste has gathered.
Like plastic islands at sea?
Kind of, though much of the plastic is in really tiny pieces.

The tide's gone out and left more plastic waste.
What difference can a little guy like me make?!

When it comes to looking after the planet ...
... every little bit helps.

Though currents help move warmth and nutrients across the planet (see page 91), they can also gather trash. Over a million tons of plastic waste is spilled into the oceans every year, most from land but some from boats. Some of it ends up in patches like the **Great Pacific Garbage Patch**, the largest of them all.

What a mess!

It needs a massive clean up.

The currents keep the waste together in an area estimated to be three times the size of France. Much of the litter is plastic, which floats and is not **biodegradable**. It can take hundreds of years to decompose. It is estimated that 94 percent of the pieces of plastic are microplastics, too small to be seen with the naked eye—so the patch looks like a murky soup.

Loggerhead turtles eat plastic bags when they mistake them for jellyfish.

Other animals can become trapped in discarded fishing nets called **GHOST NETS**.

Microplastics can be swallowed by sea creatures.

Efforts are being made to remove the largest plastic pieces from the water. The best solution is to use less plastic and recycle what we have.

How to Build Your Own Island
Why are you packing, Professor?
We're moving out!

What's wrong with the lab?
I need more space for my biggest, most dangerous experiments.

So, I'm building a new lab on an artificial tropical island.
Yay!

This will be the lab, with its helicopter pad and boat launch.
And here's where we can put our sun loungers.

We could have a lemonade and ice cream bar ... and go paddling and swimming ...

On second thought, we'd never get any work done on an island.
RRIP!

In countries where there is a shortage of dry land, artificial islands have been created. The Netherlands is a flat European country. To create more space for agriculture, areas that are usually flooded have been reclaimed by building walls or **dikes** around the land and pumping out the water. These areas are called **polders**.

In Dubai, artificial islands have been created as tourist resorts. One set of islands is shaped like a palm tree, another like a map of the world. These were built by piling up tons of rocks and sand from the seabed and then surrounding the islands with a seawall.

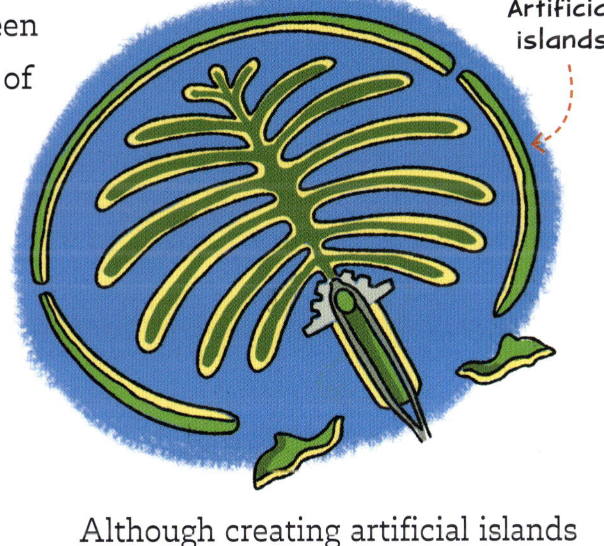

What's your artificial island made of?

Cardboard.

Although creating artificial islands provides more land for building and farming, their construction can affect the local environment, disturbing natural habitats, causing erosion, and diverting waves.

How to Catch a Wave
Are you ready for your first surfing lesson, Scooter?
I'm happy just floating.

There's a wave coming!
We have to turn the board in the same direction the wave is moving.

Start paddling in the same direction.

When you feel the board being pushed by the wave, stand up and hold a surfing pose.
Scooter?

Scooter?

Heavens Above!

(Atmosphere)

Into the Clouds

The atmosphere is the thin layer of gases that surrounds our planet. Animals need the air to breathe, while plants use gases to photosynthesize. The atmosphere also protects us from radiation from the Sun and falling space rocks. It acts like a blanket, too, trapping the Sun's heat near the Earth and keeping us warm.

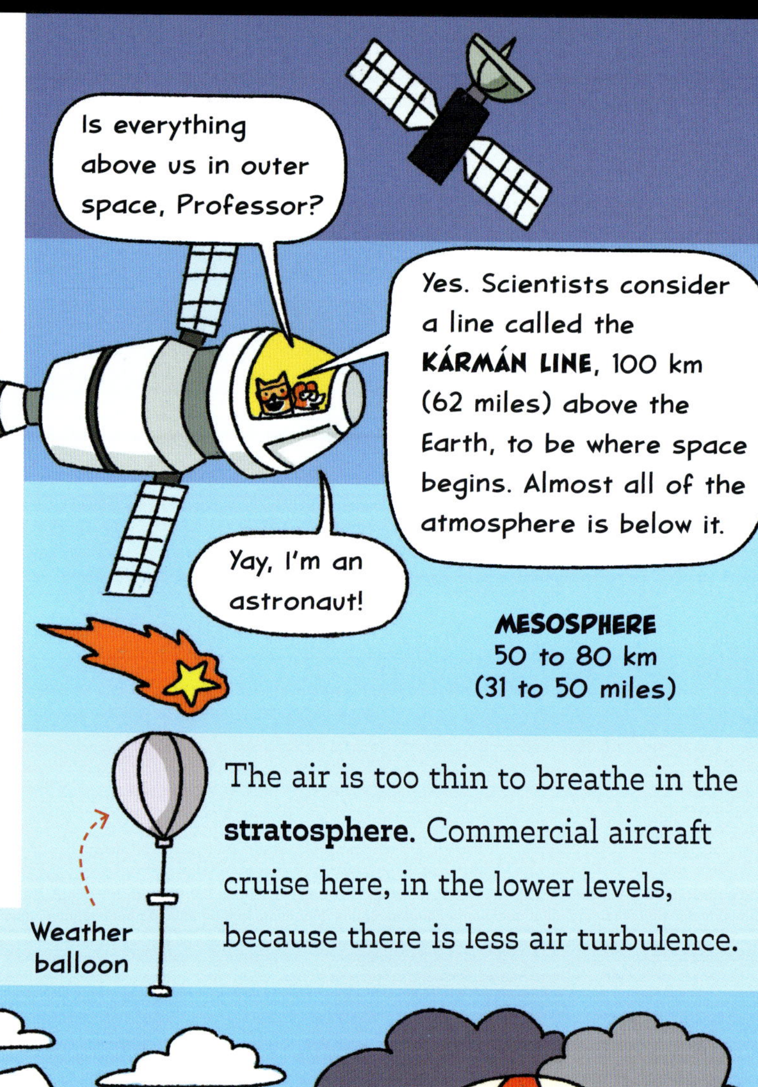

The air is too thin to breathe in the **stratosphere**. Commercial aircraft cruise here, in the lower levels, because there is less air turbulence.

EXOSPHERE
7,700 to 10,000 km
(440 to 6,200 miles)

The **exosphere** is the highest layer of the atmosphere. It's where most of Earth's artificial satellites are in orbit.

The **thermosphere** is where the thin atmosphere gets much warmer. When electrically charged particles from the Sun hit gases in the thermosphere, **aurorae** (page 17) may occur.

THERMOSPHERE
80 to 700 km
(50 to 440 miles)

The **mesosphere** is where **meteoroids** burn up as they are pulled in by Earth's gravity. It includes the coldest place on Earth, with an average temperature of -85 °C (-120 °F) near the top.

Here's where you'll find the **OZONE LAYER**.

I can't see it.

That's because it's invisible. This layer of gas protects us from harmful **ULTRAVIOLET RADIATION** from the Sun.

STRATOSPHERE
12 to 50 km
(7 to 31 miles)

The **troposphere** contains most of the air that we breathe. It is made up of the gases nitrogen (78%) and oxygen (21%), plus small amounts of argon, carbon dioxide, neon, helium, and other gases. The higher you get, the thinner the air is.

TROPOSPHERE
0 to 12 km
(0 to 7 miles)

How to Overheat the Planet
Here are your seedlings, Dr. Ringtail.
Whoa! It's warm in here!

CHUT!
This is what greenhouses are for, Scooter.
Let me close the door to keep the heat in ...

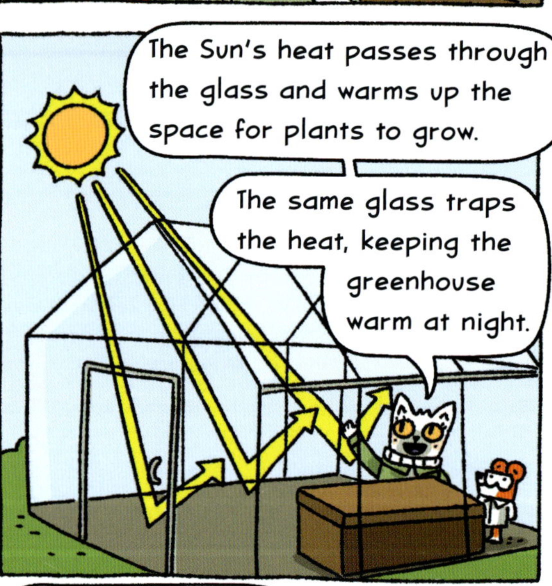
The Sun's heat passes through the glass and warms up the space for plants to grow.
The same glass traps the heat, keeping the greenhouse warm at night.

I could live in a greenhouse!
You do, in a way.
Greenhouse gases in the atmosphere trap in heat from the Sun to keep the Earth warm.

That sounds good.
Sadly, burning fossil fuels is adding too many greenhouse gases to the atmosphere, affecting Earth's climate.
At least I can walk out of this greenhouse!

Mind the d—
TUMP!

Just like a garden greenhouse, the Greenhouse Effect works by trapping in the Sun's heat.

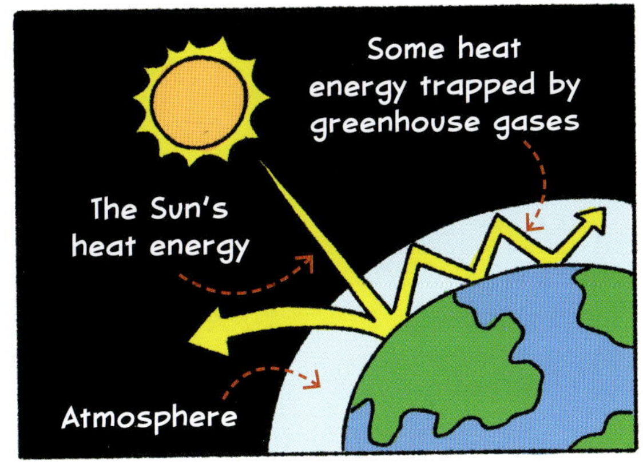

While some of the Sun's heat energy is reflected off pale surfaces such as ice and escapes through the atmosphere, some is trapped by greenhouse gases, including carbon dioxide (CO_2). These act like a blanket, keeping the Earth warm, even during the night.

While we need some greenhouse gases, the burning of fossil fuels (coal, oil, and gas) has added extra to the atmosphere. Too many greenhouse gases can have a dramatic effect on climate. Global average temperatures have been rising for decades.

Environments are changing, and deserts are growing. Ice at the poles and in glaciers is melting faster, raising sea levels and reflecting less of the Sun's heat. There are more extreme weather events such as flooding and heatwaves.

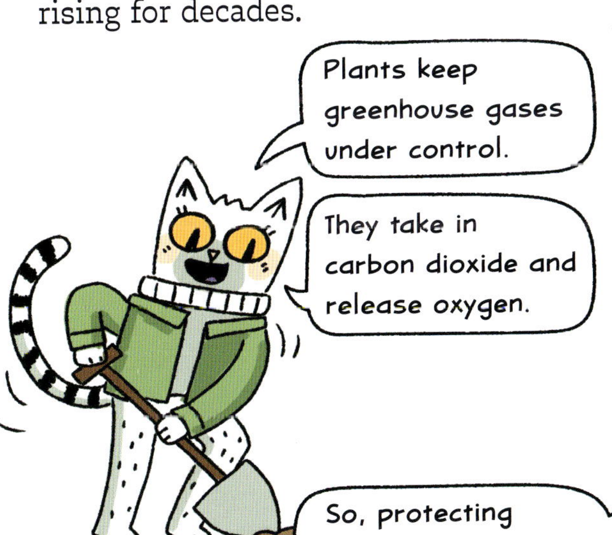

To keep greenhouse gases at a safe level, we need to reduce the use of fossil fuels and turn to renewable energy sources, such as solar, wind, and water power.

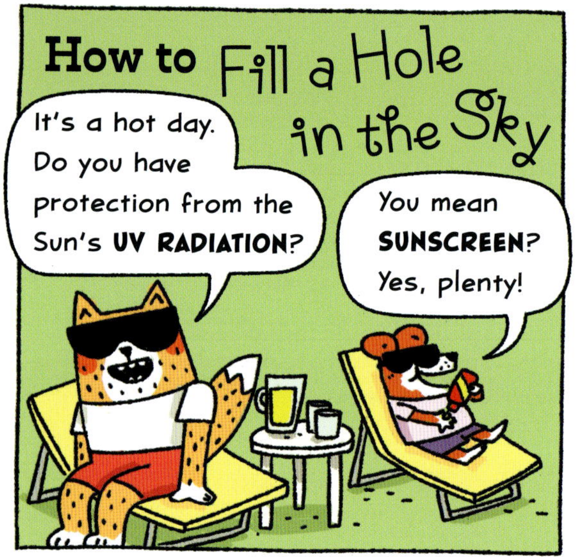
How to Fill a Hole in the Sky
It's a hot day. Do you have protection from the Sun's UV RADIATION?
You mean SUNSCREEN? Yes, plenty!

You can't rely on an OZONE LAYER to keep you safe from sunburn.
I don't have an ozone layer! I have fur.

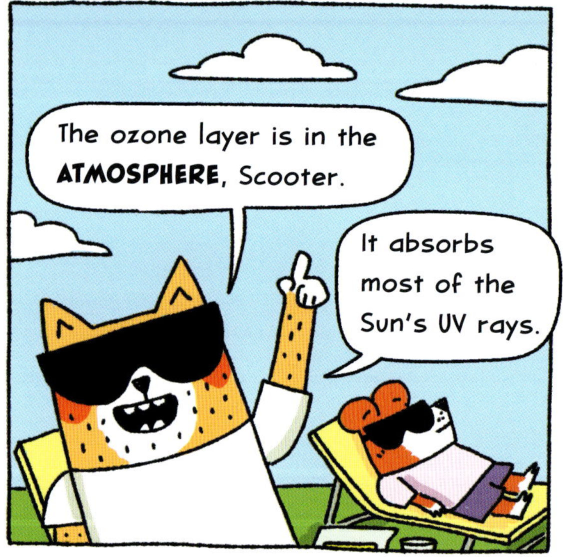
The ozone layer is in the ATMOSPHERE, Scooter.
It absorbs most of the Sun's UV rays.

Years ago, scientists discovered holes in the ozone layer.
Oh.

Holes in the sky?!

Does that mean outer space can fall in?

The **ozone layer** is a thin layer of gas in the Earth's stratosphere. Ozone is a type of oxygen and it is very important for life since it absorbs about 98 percent of the Sun's **ultraviolet (UV) radiation**.

The Sun

Ultraviolet (UV) radiation

Earth

Ozone layer

Is UV radiation bad?

While sunlight is good for us, too much UV radiation can damage the cells in our bodies and cause sunburn and even skin cancer.

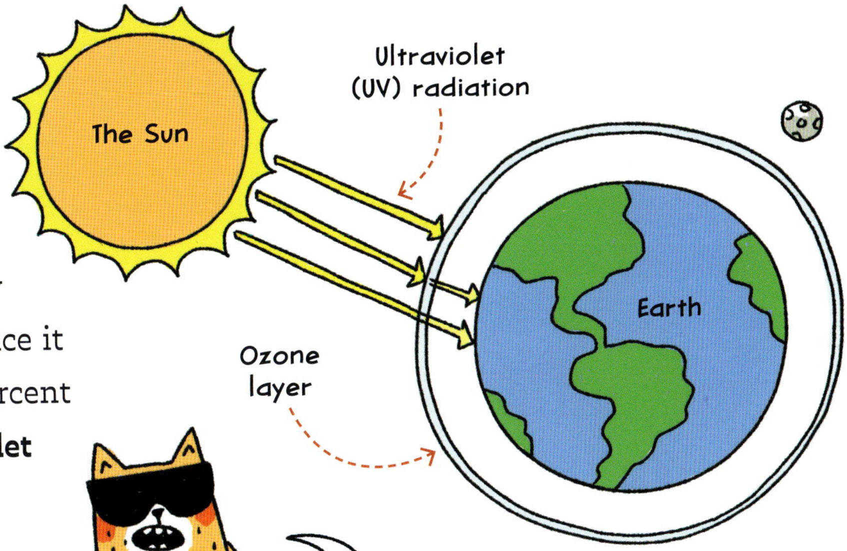

Decades ago scientists discovered areas in the sky where the ozone layer had become thinner. These were called **ozone holes.** Ozone was being lost due to the release of chemicals called **chlorofluorocarbons** or CFCs, which were used in refrigerators and aerosols.

Can we just plug the hole?

Ozone holes are not actual holes. They are areas where there is less ozone.

CFCs were outlawed. Since then, the reduction of the ozone layer has been slowed or stopped.

How to See Shapes in Clouds
What do you see when you look at that cloud, Professor?
I see an elephant!

I see a CUMULUS.
What's that?
A type of cloud.

What about this? I see a fish!
I see a STRATUS.

Can't you see animals in the clouds?!
I'm just saying what I see.
Now, I see a bunny.

Time to leave!
It's just a bunny!
It's also a CUMULONIMBUS ...

... a thundercloud!

All the clouds in the sky are made of water droplets or ice crystals so light that they float in the air. When these join together and become heavy enough, they fall as rain, hail, or snow. Knowing about clouds can help you predict the weather.

Stratus/strato—layered

Cumulus/cumulo—puffy

Cirrus/cirro—wispy

Nimbus/nimbo—rainy

So what is a **CIRROCUMULUS** cloud?

It's a wispy and puffy cloud.

High-level clouds above 6,000 m (20,000 ft).

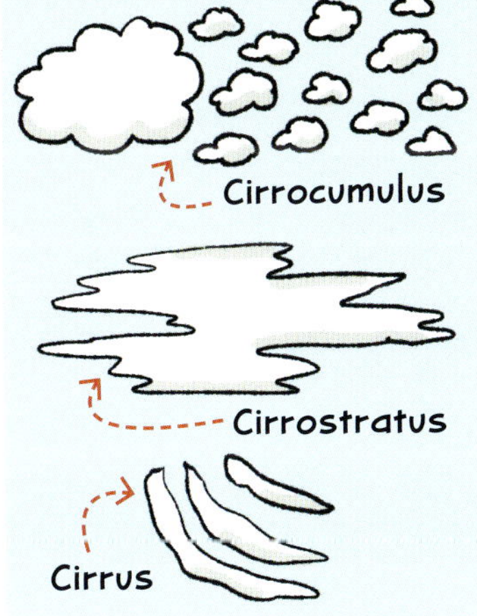

Mid-level clouds between 2,000 and 6,000 m (6,500-20,000 ft).

Nimbostratus

Altostratus

Altocumulus

Altostratus and nimbostratus can mean continuous rain or snow.

Low-level clouds below 2,000 m (6,500 ft).

Stratocumulus

Cumulonimbus

Cumulus

Stratus

There's a cloud that looks like me!

Cumulus are fluffy clouds like balls of cotton that appear with fair weather. Stratus are low-level sheets that can cover hills like fog. Cumulonimbus are tall thunderclouds.

How to Predict the Weather
Well, what do you think?
It looks complicated, so I guess you're happy.

I am! This is my new WEATHER STATION.
This is the HYGROMETER which measure HUMIDITY.

This RAIN GAUGE measures how much rain has fallen.
The THERMOMETER ...
I know this one! It measures TEMPERATURE!

The BAROMETER measures air pressure ...
... and the ANEMOMETER measures wind speed.

All of this helps me record and predict the weather.

I bet you didn't predict that!
CLONK!

The weather is what we call Earth's changing atmospheric conditions, the result of the Sun's energy warming the land and sea. The land warms up more quickly than water, heating the air above it. This creates differences in air pressure, causing air movement from areas of high to low pressure.

High-pressure systems are areas of cool, dry air that prevent moist air rising to form clouds. This usually means clear skies and fine weather.

Low-pressure systems are areas of warm, damp air that result in clouds, rain, or snow.

Warm air

High pressure

Cold air

Low pressure

When warm air moves into an area of cold air, this is called a **warm front**. When cold air moves into an area of warm air, this is called a **cold front**. Weather fronts appear on a map like this.

H

L

H—high pressure

L—low pressure

Warm front—

Cold front—

The forecast today is lots and lots of weather!

The weather is described by six main measurements:

- Temperature
- Atmospheric pressure
- Wind speed and direction
- Humidity, how moist it feels
- Precipitation, such as rain or snow
- Cloudiness

How to Get Blown Off Your Feet
Why do we need to wear these heavy boots?
These are my specially designed ANTI-HURRICANE BOOTS.

They will make you too heavy to be blown away by strong wind.
What strong wind?

THIS strong wind! A HURRICANE is approaching, as forecast.

We should get away!
It's more powerful than I expected.

I can't run in these heavy boots!
Me neither!

You might need to rethink your anti-hurricane boots.

Hurricanes, **typhoons**, and **cyclones** are powerful tropical storms that can spin at speeds up to 400 km/h (250 mph). The storms have different names depending on where they form. Hurricanes appear in the Caribbean and North America, typhoons around China and Japan, while cyclones happen in the Indian Ocean.

Rain clouds

Warm, humid air

Spinning winds

Low pressure

Warm ocean, over 27 °C (80 °F) at the surface

All this information is making my head spin!

The storms form when warm air rises over the ocean to create clouds. The warm air is replaced by cold air that heats up and rises, too, forming storm clouds that spin due to Earth's rotation. The storms can bring devastating wind and heavy rains to coastal areas, ripping up buildings and trees.

How to Leave the Doldrums
It's no good, the sails are not picking up any wind.
We're in the **DOLDRUMS**.

The doldrums?
This is an area near the equator where there might not be wind for weeks.

Weeks?! We'll run out of food and water.
I already ate the last choc-chip muffin!

There's only one thing we can do ...
It's OK, Professor. I'll sacrifice myself ...

Don't be silly, Scooter.
I mean we can turn on the **ENGINE**.
BRMMM!

Why didn't you say we had an engine?!

The Sun heats different parts of the planet at different rates. This causes differences in air temperature and pressure. As hot air rises, it leaves an area of low pressure which is filled by denser cold air. This movement creates wind patterns in Earth's lower atmosphere.

The wind is strongest over water where there are no trees, hills, or buildings in the way to slow it down.

There are five major wind zones across the Earth: the **polar easterlies**, **westerlies**, **horse latitudes**, **trade winds**, and the **doldrums**.

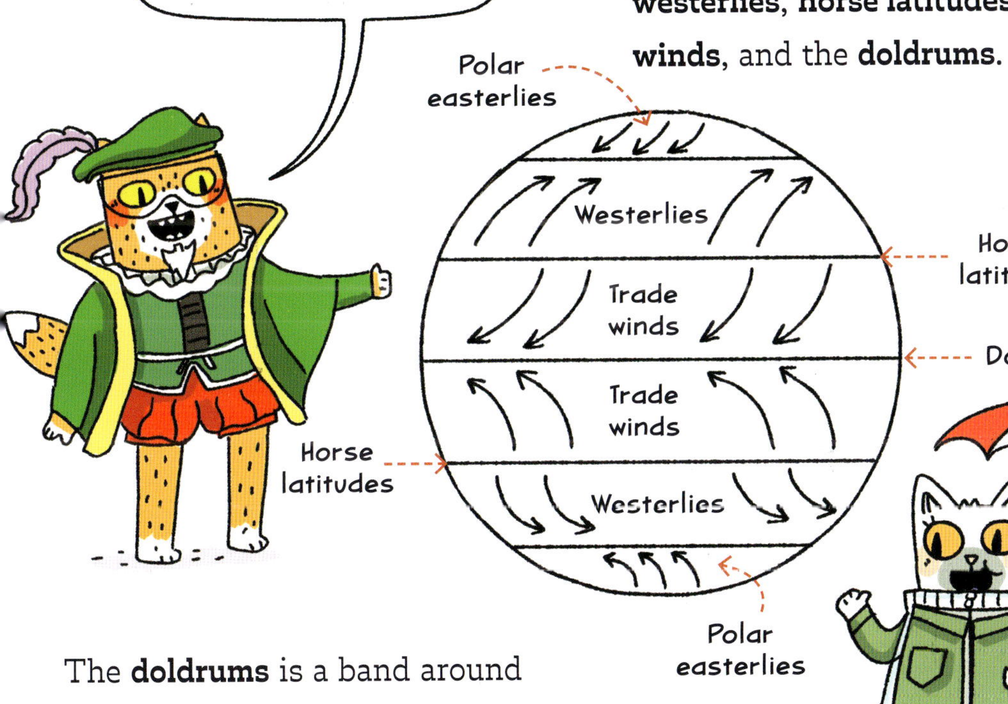

The **doldrums** is a band around Earth's equator where warm, moist air rises to form clouds and rain. Since the air moves upward, there is little wind, so sailboats can be trapped for weeks.

The **MONSOON**, which brings dry weather or heavy rain to Southeast Asia, is a trade wind.

How to Chase a Tornado

Are tornadoes dangerous?
While some tornadoes can last for seconds, some last hours, traveling many kilometers at speeds up to 480 km/h (300 mph).
They can rip up anything in their path.

Why would we want to get close to something like that?
It's science, Scooter! We can learn so much by studying the weather directly.

I'm getting strong readings.
A tornado passed through here not long ago.

You THINK?!

Perhaps you're right. We should get out of here fast.
How fast?

As fast as the wind!

How to Soak Up the Sun
Oh dear.
What's up, Scooter?
My phone's run out of power.

Why don't you use some of the Sun's energy?
I can't plug my phone into the Sun!

It's too far away ... and the cable would probably melt.
You don't need to visit the Sun! The Sun's light and heat energy reaches Earth.

We can collect some of this energy using solar panels and convert it into electricity.
These are too big to put in my pocket.

Not all solar panels are huge. I have one on my backpack.
I'm going to order one of those for myself!

Oh dear.
What's up, Scooter?
My phone's run out of power.

Energy from the Sun keeps the Earth warm and is responsible for changing weather patterns. It can also be used as a source of **renewable energy**. **Solar panels** are devices designed to capture the Sun's energy. Sunlight shines on **photovoltaic cells** in the panels, which convert this into electricity to heat homes and power devices.

Solar panels can be placed on rooftops or in fields in what are called **solar farms**. Unlike fossil fuels, such as oil and gas, solar energy is a **renewable energy source** that is cleaner, and it doesn't run out.

How to Get Your Own Storm
And Storm Robert will bring strong winds to the east coast on Friday ...
Storm Robert?

Why do storms have names?
It's just so they can be identified.

Names are picked in alphabetical order. Some years, the storms are given boys' names, some years girls' names.
Can I get a storm named after me?

I suppose they might run out of names beginning with S ...
Wow! I hope I'm a really big storm that stops traffic and gets on the news ...

Storm Scooter, causing chaos as he blows by ...

Storm Scooter, could you go back and clean up your chaos?

Major storms are given names so they can easily be identified in weather reports. The names come from official lists provided by **meteorological organizations**. There are different lists of names depending on where the storm begins.

The list of names may be repeated every few years, but if a large and dangerous storm happens, its name may not be used again. Hurricane Ida in 2021 was one of the most destructive in history. The name Ida has now been retired, along with Katrina, Tracy, Sandy, and Haiyan.

Weather satellites track storms developing in tropical regions. Reports are shared from ships and planes, too, so early warnings can be given and people can take shelter or evacuate from regions at risk.

How to Build the Perfect Snowman
My snowman is no good.
It keeps crumbling away.

This snow is too dry. That's why it doesn't stick together.

This snow is wetter ... and better!

Good for snowballs, too!
Hey!

Now, to build a good snowman, you need to roll a large ball for a body.
Like this ...

Scooter?
Scooter, are you watching?

Rain forms when the tiny water droplets in clouds gather around tiny dust particles. They merge and become too heavy to float in the air. When it's cold enough, these tiny drops of water become **ice crystals**. These build up and fall to the ground. If they do not melt on the way down, they land as **snow**.

Snowflakes are always hexagonal, or six-sided, due to the structure of the ice crystals.

Sleet is a mix of snow and rain, icy drops that melt as they fall to the ground.

Hail is formed when frost sticks to the ice crystals to make icy pellets. These are lifted higher in the cloud by air currents, and they collect more ice before falling to the ground as hailstones. Some can be the size of golf balls.

How to
Avoid an
Avalanche
It's hard w—
Shhh!

What's th—
Shhh!

Whisper if you have to say anything, and step gently.
Vibrations can set off an avalanche.
AN AVALA—

Mmmph!
Yes, an avalanche.
Tons of snow can come tumbling down off the mountaintops.
We'd be buried!

What's that noise?
TOK TOK
TOK
TOK

Sorry. That's my knees trembling.

An **avalanche** is a large mass of snow, ice, and rock that suddenly slides down a mountain. The fall can be triggered by thawing, a fresh snowfall, an earthquake, snow sliding off layers of ice, or vibrations.

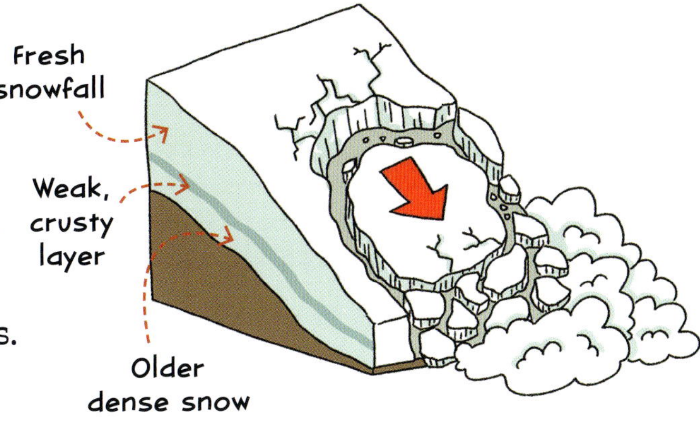

A **slough avalanche** is one made up of powdery snow. A **slab avalanche** is one where a large block of compressed snow breaks free. This type is the most dangerous.

The avalanche picks up speed and material as it falls. The material in a large avalanche can weigh up to a million tons. It can descend much faster than a skier, so it is hard to escape from it.

In some skiing areas, explosives are set off before the start of the skiing season to remove loose snow from the peaks.

If you're below an avalanche, you need to hurry to the side, away from falling snow, or reach a tree. If covered by snow, swim to the surface quickly before the snow hardens.

How to Save the Future
Super-Scooter arrives in time to save the planet!
Super-Scooter fills in the ozone hole!
Next, Super-Scooter blows out a raging forest fire. Awesome!
Now, Super-Scooter sucks in greenhouse gases, to keep Earth from overheating.
S
Hooray! Super-Scooter scoops up plastics from the ocean.
Super-Scooter puts cardboard into the recycling bin.
Great job, Scooter! Keep on saving the planet!

The use of fossil fuels is adding greenhouse gases to the atmosphere. Forests are being cut down for wood and to make way for farms. Plastics and other long-lasting materials are being dumped in the environment. But, there are many ways we can help reduce the damage.

Don't waste food and water.
Just eat and use what you need. Think about where your food comes from, and avoid unnecessary packaging.

Walk, bicycle, and use public transportation.
Planes and most cars burn fossil fuels. Take public transportation or, if the journey is short, bicycle or walk.

Reduce waste. Reuse, repair, and recycle.
So much waste ends up in landfill. Avoid adding to the problem by buying less and making what you have last longer. When you no longer want something, you can donate or recycle it.

Go wild.
Plants take the greenhouse gas carbon dioxide from the air and replace it with the oxygen. Plant more, and let green areas grow a little wilder to provide a home for wildlife.

Index